ALLEGRA
HICKS

AN EYE
FOR
DESIGN

ALLEGRA HICKS

AN EYE
FOR
DESIGN

CREATIVE DIRECTION BY ANTONIO MONFREDA

PHOTOGRAPHY BY EMANUELE MASCIONI

WRITTEN WITH NOGA ARIKHA

FOREWORD BY PATRICK KINMONTH

ABRAMS, NEW YORK

FOR ANGELICA AND AMBROSIA

EDITOR: REBECCA KAPLAN

DESIGNER: KWASI OSEI

COVER DESIGN: MICHELLE ISHAY-COHEN

PRODUCTION MANAGER: ANKUR GHOSH

Library of Congress Cataloging-in-Publication Data

Hicks, Allegra.

Allegra Hicks : an eye for design / Allegra Hicks with Noga Arihka.

    p. cm.

Includes bibliographical references and index.

ISBN 978-0-8109-9573-4 (alk. paper)

1. Hicks, Allegra—Themes, motives. 2. Interior decoration—England. 3.

Design—England. I. Arihka, Noga. II. Title.

NK2047.6.H52A4 2010

747—dc22

2010011120

Printed and bound in Hong Kong, China

10 9 8 7 6 5 4 3 2 1

Abrams books are available at special discounts when purchased in quantity for premiums and promotions
as well as fundraising or educational use. Special editions can also be created to specification. For details,
contact specialmarkets@abramsbooks.com or the address below.

THE ART OF BOOKS SINCE 1949

115 West 18th Street
New York, NY 10011
www.abramsbooks.com

CONTENTS

FOREWORD

Last autumn in Rome, I met Allegra Hicks. I knew her prints and textiles, of course, but above all I knew her eye. She has applied her way of seeing to many things, from the clothes of some of my best-dressed girlfriends, to the interiors of the houses they wear them in. On my travels, I have often noticed that the key thing in a room I like has been made, chosen, or designed by her. Allegra's work seems always to bring a modernity with it that understands and speaks eloquently to the past. And yet, her designs have a distinct and original voice.

We spoke of many things, what lies behind these bold and elegant designs and how her life has nurtured her eye for pattern. It transpired that she was making a book about her work, collaborating with our mutual friend with impeccable taste, Antonio Monfreda. Afterward, they wondered if our conversation might prove to be the basis of some kind of introduction, since the book was designed to tell its story through pictures, and to be an inspiration rather than a polemic. And so, by applying the method they had evolved for the book, I have collaged our thoughts from that original conversation and stitched in ideas from other days spent together. In doing this, I have attempted to weave my own swatch of ideas for Allegra (if only to act as a lining for hers), following the bright threads of her inspiration and the glance of a remarkable designer's eye.

—PATRICK KINMONTH
BERLIN, 2009

As a small child,
my parents
taught me to
look at things.
Not just to see
the world around me,
but to be conscious
understanding it.
In other words
they taught me how
to appreciate
beauty.

The first time I became aware of seeing something in this way was when I was about five, in the Picasso Museum in Antibes. I became fascinated by a line Picasso had drawn and saw that a line could be made to describe something better than words. Of course, as a child, you have to draw a hundred lines in order to approximate what you want to say, because you hardly know how to speak in any language. So I was shocked to see that, with just one line, Picasso had said everything he wanted to say. It was a picture of a dove, not a masterpiece perhaps, but astonishing to me.

Famously, many people said of Picasso at the time, "A child could do it. . . . " But the point is rather that a child could understand it, because Picasso's art speaks the language of the child through the adult eye. I suppose that I was learning to draw, myself, and the dove was done with a crayon or a pastel, the kind of thing a child uses . . . but for whatever reason it stayed with me, and what it awakened has never slept since.

The next step for me was seeing how lines can become a block of color and what happens then. You draw and draw until the lines eventually make a block. I saw the different power a block of color has, even in two dimensions, and how it is influenced by the space around it. It was something I discovered by feeling, rather than as something explained, very early on. It fascinated me then and it still does. And that first sensation is really the basis of all my subsequent work.

Meanwhile, I was living with my resolutely modern parents. We had strange cutlery that didn't look like anyone else's, and I loved how it would amaze my school friends. We had a glass dining table, which nobody else in Turin had. That meant that my younger sister and I really had to be incredibly well behaved, as you couldn't make a mess or drop your food under the table. We had things designed by Gio Ponti and Albini, glass by Venini. All the things around us were of the time—it was the sixties in Italy, and a new vision about how to live was emerging in that amazing country saturated with the past. Just as in England after the war, although probably for very different cultural reasons, there was a longing among my parents' generation to turn a new page in the way things looked.

My father is a physicist and a musician, but design was equally important to him. He collaborated on our new Turin house with his chosen architect when I was about eight. He found a bit of land on the hill outside the city where, eventually, this extraordinary place was built. It used as much glass as possible and looked at the mountains. There were moving panels to separate the bedrooms, and it was open plan. At night, there were terrifying shadows of trees everywhere, and I imagined every sort of horror lurking out there. Just getting to the bathroom was a great adventure. But it was a beautiful house.

My mother was passionate about design, too, and had a great love of literature and the theater, so between them my parents immersed my sister and I in art and design in a completely relaxed way. I only discovered later that this was remotely unusual. The sounds of Bach—the Goldberg

Variations—Schumann, Debussy, and Ravel filled the house from my earliest days. And I used to see the music in terms of color as much as anything, imagining the colors changing with the different energy of the music. It was just part of life.

This idea of art and life being fused harmoniously together has shaped my work. I let designs evolve out of pleasure, out of seeing something that I find inspiring and beautiful. There is no aggression or violence in a pattern when I finally find it (although those can be part of the process of getting a design fully realized!). Looking at Matisse taught me a lot, too—especially the way in which he used color and line to communicate the joy he felt in looking at the world around him. So I really thank my parents for giving us this background, since, of course, feeling that artistic things are natural does not just encourage you to create; it also gives you something deeply as a person . . . a sort of affinity with harmony.

I went to the Liceo Classico, which, as my mother said, was a proper education. She knew Latin and ancient Greek, recited Homer at length by heart, and could not imagine that I would not want to do the same. It was only after I had finished at the Liceo that I could understand what she had been talking about. Now I do recognize that a classical education offers a particularly rich way of understanding and thinking about the modern world, and I have always given a prayer of thanks to my mother for sending me on that terribly unfashionable but marvelous path. It teaches you a profound sense of beauty.

Our Greek teacher was a psychoanalyst and a wonderfully sympathetic character. I remember him coming to the class with drums to beat out the rhythms of Pindar's odes. Education at that level is as much about the teacher as the subject. An inspired teacher like him can alter your path for a lifetime.

I have always had a natural interest in and love for color. At art school in Milan, we made the colors ourselves from scratch before we were allowed to paint with them, and it was always my job to prepare them for the class. I found I could match any color that was needed, in the way that a perfumer knows how to deconstruct a scent and put its ingredients back together again. In Brussels, we used eggs and beer as the medium for the paints. We were taught to use beer to prepare a plastered wall for fresco; it removes the oiliness that makes a surface refuse the pigment. If you wash the wall with beer first and then use beer with the pigment, it makes a perfect fixative.

While living in London, I met and married Ashley Hicks. Through his father, the renowned British designer David Hicks, Ashley had been breathing design from birth and was always surrounded by the very best of it. Although he grew up under the hugely powerful influence of his father, he had found his own way. I realized at this time that something crucial was missing from my life: my own language. I had been drawing all day long for hours at a time, always patterns, but I had no idea how they should be applied.

India has been fundamental to my work. In the months after I returned from my first visit, I kept seeing the patterns of India emerging from my memory onto the painted page. And the primary motifs have stayed with me to this day. Of course, almost all decorative languages of ornament come from looking at plants—from the acanthus leaves of Corinthian capitals to Egyptian columns in the shape of lotus buds. But I wanted to return to the most basic forms of the seeds and origins of plant forms. Indian motifs always have a powerful and beautiful abstract element that goes back to the roots of design. An almond shape I drew became my starting point, my A; I turned this over and with a dot added above it, it was my B. Eventually, I had a complete alphabet of shapes I loved that I tentatively started to use to speak my own language.

From there I found my way to aboriginal paintings, always getting closer and deeper into nature, as if looking at a leaf through a microscope, finding the shapes of a single cell, and getting to the essence of a shape.

During the start of my business, I felt the need to try to express my soul, to paint and draw for its own sake. I set my sights very high, perhaps too high. I was terrified and horrified about doing this. Totally exposing oneself that way seemed so brutal. And having looked so much at the old masters of art, I felt the weight of history and the fabulous work that had been done for centuries as a judge and jury looking over my shoulder. But when I used what I knew to make design rather than art, the clouds lifted, and I felt both liberated and at one with the process: The results started to give me pleasure rather than pain.

Really good designers have no inhibition about the depth of pleasure that taste can give both to them and to others. But taste is a hugely complex issue in painting. Good taste has traditionally been seen as the death of good art. The word "decorative," for a painter, is usually a term of abuse. Although in some recent contemporary art, decoration has emerged as a new frontier for fine artists, they are often using it with conscious irony as a kind of kitsch. For me, great decorative work has the power to move me as profoundly as a masterpiece by a great painter; its success is based on pleasure. The best taste is not bland, of course. It can be a challenge and very intense, but the result is uplifting. If your consciousness goes in a different direction, decoration can allow you to connect with your subconscious without worrying that what you are saying is unoriginal. Decoration welcomes both reference and tradition.

When I went back to India, I became interested in block printing, not really knowing whether I wanted to make a dress or a print. I was most fascinated by the idea of the fabric itself. Through my experience with rugmaking in the past, I had become bewitched by the processes involved in making an idea become a reality, the alchemy of it. I found the whole sequence of events magical. You have a thought, then you draw it, and then you pass it through someone else's skill, and it evolves, becomes concrete, a thing in itself with a separate life.

I had a drawing of an idea for a pattern and went to see an old man, a block cutter, who drew my idea on the wood and cut the block. After a faltering conversation, because my Hindi was as poor as his English, somehow within a few hours we were printing my first pattern on light cotton. Lengths were hanging to dry in the sun, the colors looking very different, actually changing as they dried. The craftsmen and women were so kind to me. They started looking at and discussing the patterns, often suggesting names for those they liked. One was a shape derived from Portuguese printing. "Oh," they said, "it's lovely. It looks like Kali's eyebrows." (Kali is the goddess of time and change.) So the print has been called Kali ever since. Another reminded them of Genghis Khan's mustache so, of course, that one had to be called Mouskan.

Two-dimensional design can take you into the dimension of dreams, not just the third, but also the fourth, fifth, and sixth dimensions. I love to investigate the illusion of depth on a flat surface. There are so many stories that can be told with motif and pattern—embroidered, woven, printed, or in combination. It's an endless tale.

The Japanese kimono is probably the supreme example of clothing that exhibits the interplay of shape and storytelling through the material, the surface, and the pattern of the fabric. I love the kimono's ability to transcend fashion while embodying a culture at the same time. The fact that the kimono has evolved over centuries, and continues to evolve even now, is its finest testimonial. The biggest compliment anyone could pay me is that they feel I have made something that is more a matter of culture than of fashion. That is my goal, even if that means that my clothing might not be able to define an era as fashion often can.

I feel that the way one can put all these thoughts together in the most inspiring and concrete way of all is in interiors. A room can define an era as much as the clothes worn in it or those who inhabit it. A harmoniously decorated room embodies the spirit of its owners and creators, like a self-portrait. A very well-designed room evokes and involves all the senses, from the visual to the physical. And the scent of a room can be as powerful as its colors and shapes: the old consoling smell of leather books in a library, or a room of velvet where wood fires have been frequently lit, or a room where there is a jasmine or wisteria flowering outside so that the scent, the place, and the memory of time spent there all fuse together. A color, a texture, or a pattern can become very personal, like a Proustian key to a place in one's memory. And the places we have chosen to put together in this book are all touchstones of this kind for me. I can effortlessly see them with my inner eye. They are my constant companions, my inspiration, and are crucial to my work as a designer.

—FROM CONVERSATIONS BETWEEN ALLEGRA HICKS AND PATRICK KINMONTH

INTRODUCTION

This book retraces the genesis of the patterns I have created over the past decades. When I began to work as a designer—after finishing my studies, during which time I learned a variety of techniques—I had to find my own vocabulary. And I started by looking at nature. Patterns are always an elaboration of nature, a microcosm that takes off from shapes in the macrocosm. I observed everything that is part of our everyday life, searching for the essence of these things. I still work in this way. Out of the observation of the world, there emerges an abstraction, a pattern, which finds its own life once I remove it from its original context.

Seasons, on the other hand, and the colors associated with them, deeply affect the senses; in turn, and partly for that reason, designs are adapted to each season. And so dividing the book into seasons seemed the best way to tell my story, by following in the most natural way the inherent seasonality of the collections themselves. Seasons are deeply sensorial, sensual phenomena we experience through variations in light, temperature, humidity, smells, tastes; and to each season corresponds its equally sensorial textiles, colors, and patterns. I wanted to bring to the fore this deep correspondence between fabric and season, united as these are by the senses. The five senses condition our lives, and our creative lives all the more. This awareness of the centrality of sense experience has informed my emotional and creative vocabulary, and it is the basis of my design ethos and aesthetics. We don't only use our eyes when we contemplate a fabric, but all our senses. The textile will have a texture we touch, and its feel may trigger a host of associations: Its colors and patterns may suggest states of mind, with their own smells and tastes; its rustle will have its particular, subtle sound.

A friend of mine, Antonio Monfreda, with whom I share a lot of my aesthetic, heard about what I was doing, and through his very inspiring suggestions he became the creative director of this book. He has always been aware of how strongly pictorial my work is. "Allegra's fabrics are akin to paintings and watercolors," he said. "I remember how, some fifteen years ago, I witnessed her casually making gorgeous watercolors of fabrics while speaking on the telephone and thinking about her next dress, rug, or console." The focus of the book, he thought, "should be the fabrics, of which there is an immense, highly original production: not the clothes, or the interior design, but the stuff of which these are made. This seems the best way to do justice to the fierce independence of vision that characterizes Allegra's work." When Monfreda took rough pictures of the fabrics, with a simple digital camera, he realized that we should focus on the pictorial aspect of the fabrics, and we decided that the final pictures should be out-of-focus, so as to emphasize the fabrics' abiding sensuality.

The seasonality of the fabrics was beautifully translated by the pictures, in the way in which each one suggests a climate, a setting, a mood, by way of texture, color, pattern, and so on. From there, it made sense to pair the fabrics with their sources, be they in nature, interiors, or quirky details from my travels in England or India, Tuscany or New York. Throughout the book, the fabrics are thus juxtaposed with images that, at first, may look unrelated to them, but are in fact an important part of their story. The associations are suggestive; the fabric may be the strong element in one set, the interior or landscape may be the strong one in another. But throughout, there is a back-and-forth between inspiration and outcome—between objects, rooms, houses, gardens, and various places in the world, and the fabrics that emerge out of them.

These juxtapositions are meant to inspire, to encourage the reader to see the fabrics as the mental landscapes that they are, and to envision the landscapes as potential fabrics. The book is an internal voyage through someone's mind, shaped so as to let the reader bounce off the images and texts, and look at design in a novel way.

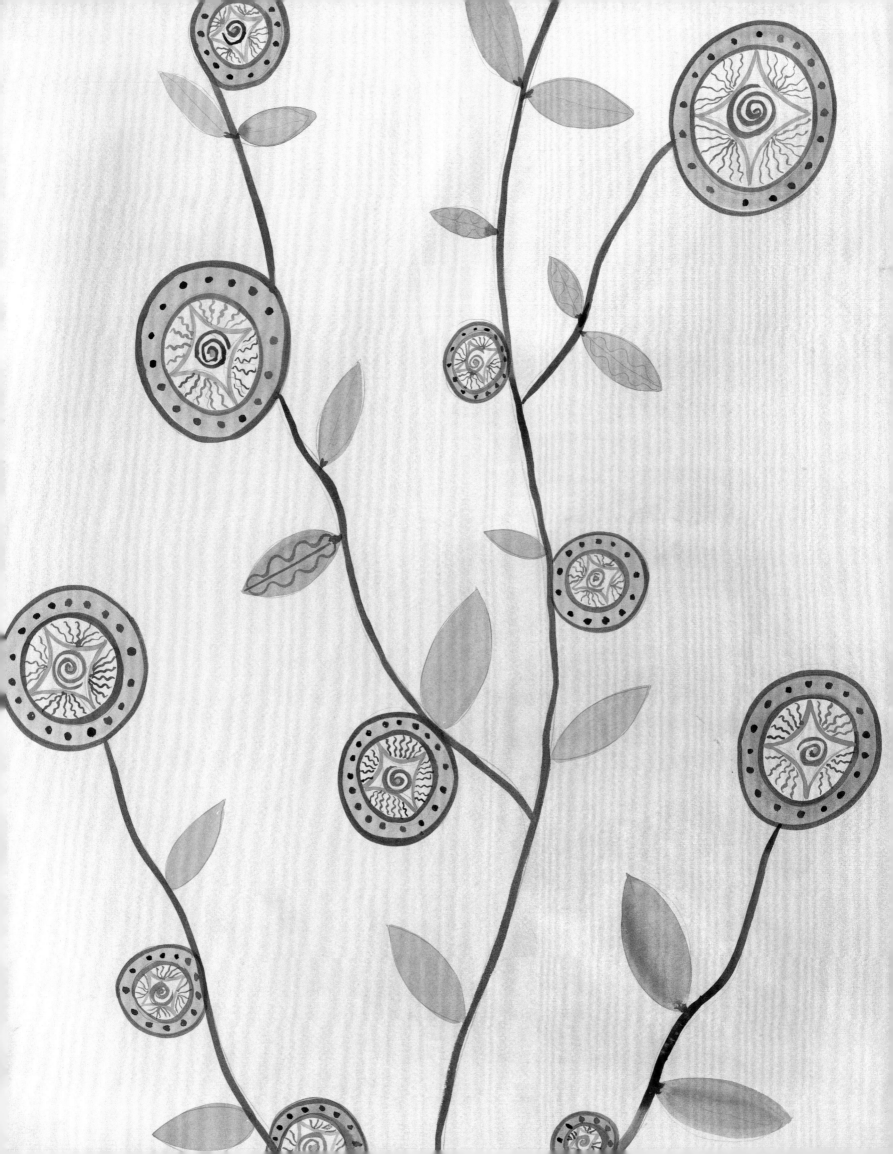

SPRING

IS A
TIME OF
GENTLENESS,
WHEN NATURE
SLOWLY
ROUSES ITSELF
FROM DEEP SLEEP
AND THE SENSES
AWAKE. IT IS A TIME
OF REBIRTH, AND
THIS JOYOUS,
FRESH BEGINNING
IS WHAT I WANT TO
CONVEY VISUALLY IN
SPRING FABRICS.

From the
black-and-white
of winter emerges
a variegated
palette of greens
and soft colors
suggestive of
the joys of spring
and of the shades
water takes
during this
season.

Colors are muted, but they have a hint of a strong pigment, such as the sky and sea that strive to become turquoise, and the sun that strives to be yellow. A bit of wintry sleepiness remains in the cooler pigments, and it is as if the fabric were paper painted with a light brush, mixing pigment and water. In effect, spring feels like a watercolor.

The sense of gentle spring can be achieved on jute, chiffon, silk, cotton, or linen. Because spring is an anticipation of summer, it calls for light textiles that adorn rather than cover the body. The spring mood is serene, the space full of promise, the atmosphere one of expectation. When creating a fabric, I achieve a springlike mood principally by adopting an ease, or looseness, in the pattern, and a freedom in the modulation of shape and color, which beckon and guide but do not assert too forcefully. The pattern flows in a melodic way, leading one on a harmonious path, as if one were strolling and humming along a river on a bright, brisk morning; spring is the most melodic of all the seasons. There is a light, adolescent feel to this season. It is a time of beginnings, when one wants to find out what will come next—a time of youth, of a new, gentle warmth perpetually refreshed by water.

Spring colors emerge on the fabrics in the same way as the season itself: The darkness of winter has been left behind, but some of it still lingers. Softer and lighter colors look as if they are painted on a darker ground. It is important to acknowledge where spring comes from: Darkness helps define light and indicates the origin of life. The colors and patterns suggest the passage of dark to light and of cold to warm; they translate movement, curiosity, and freshness. Water is also central because it changes with each season. It is very different in spring from what it is in winter: From its frozen state, it becomes a little stream, a trickle, and a source of new life. The fabric translates the sense that water is congenial, refreshing, musical, and no longer associated with long nights and cold days. The patterns contain this life-giving metamorphosis in the way they freely unfold and are colored with happy blues, fulfilling turquoise, and new greens.

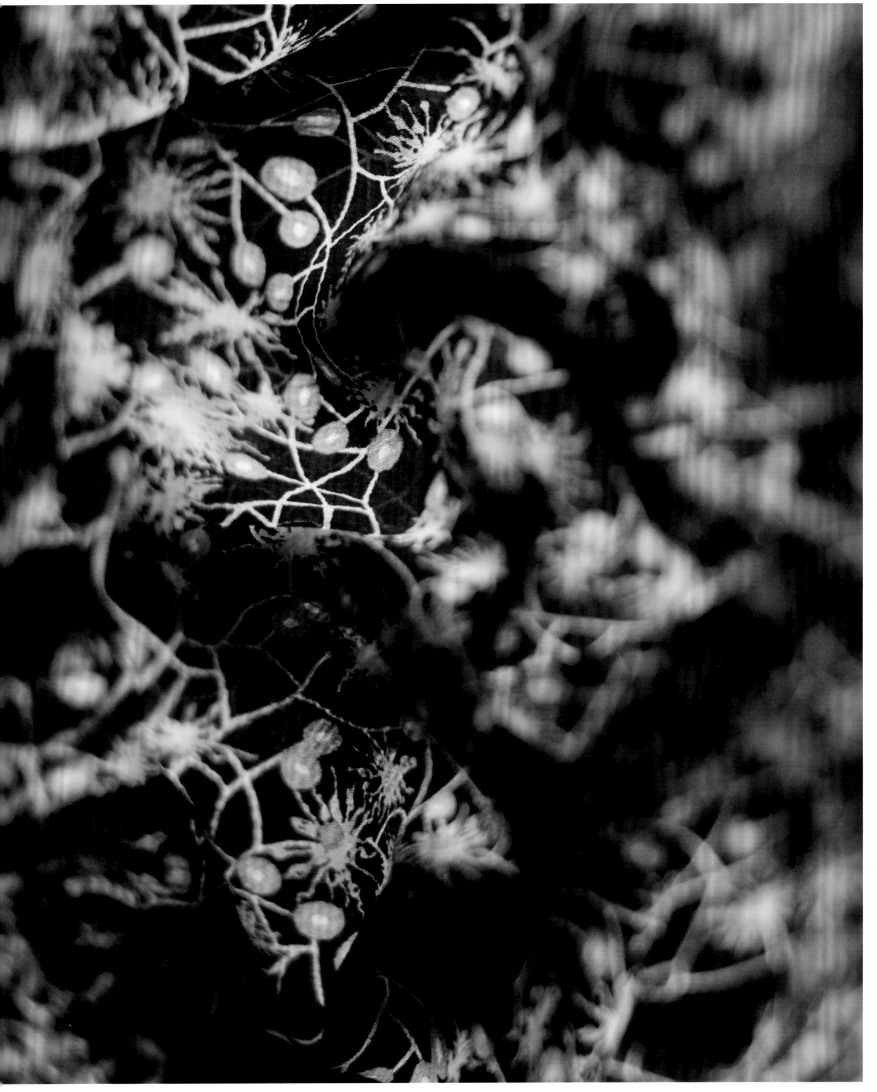

GARDENS

The world of color is not just a visual experience; it captures all the senses. Colors evoke emotions, memories, moments, and places. They can be associated with smells and sensations of all kinds. In the spring, I avoid primary colors. I deliberately mix shades that allow the eye to pick out what it wants from what it sees, that let the brain select and perform its color-coding magic. Primary colors impose themselves and enclose the imagination; they don't let the eye create the chromatic world. I want the world to be created by the eye, through colored patterns. I have found inspiration in Italianate gardens; their geometry and symmetry create repeating patterns of color and shape that readily translate to fabric design. There are blues for sky and greens for vegetation, and there is white, because in a pattern one needs a noncolor to sense which color it is one is striving for. By using these unsaturated, watery colors that are inspired by nature in springtime, I create watercolor-like patterns that have the feel of spring. In the pattern on the previous page, you can sense a stream, and drops of water; they suggest gentle motion, the subtle presence of elements that are perpetually in becoming and always being reborn into patterns, just as it is in nature. In this case, the Italianate garden is about to become colorful and ripe; its geometry is ordered, but gentle, and the whites offset the greens in a manner that is relaxing to the eye. Such a palette is perfect for an interior, for a sitting room, a drawing room, and in particular, for a bedroom; greens, blues, and whites help convey the calm and harmony that are so necessary in bedrooms.

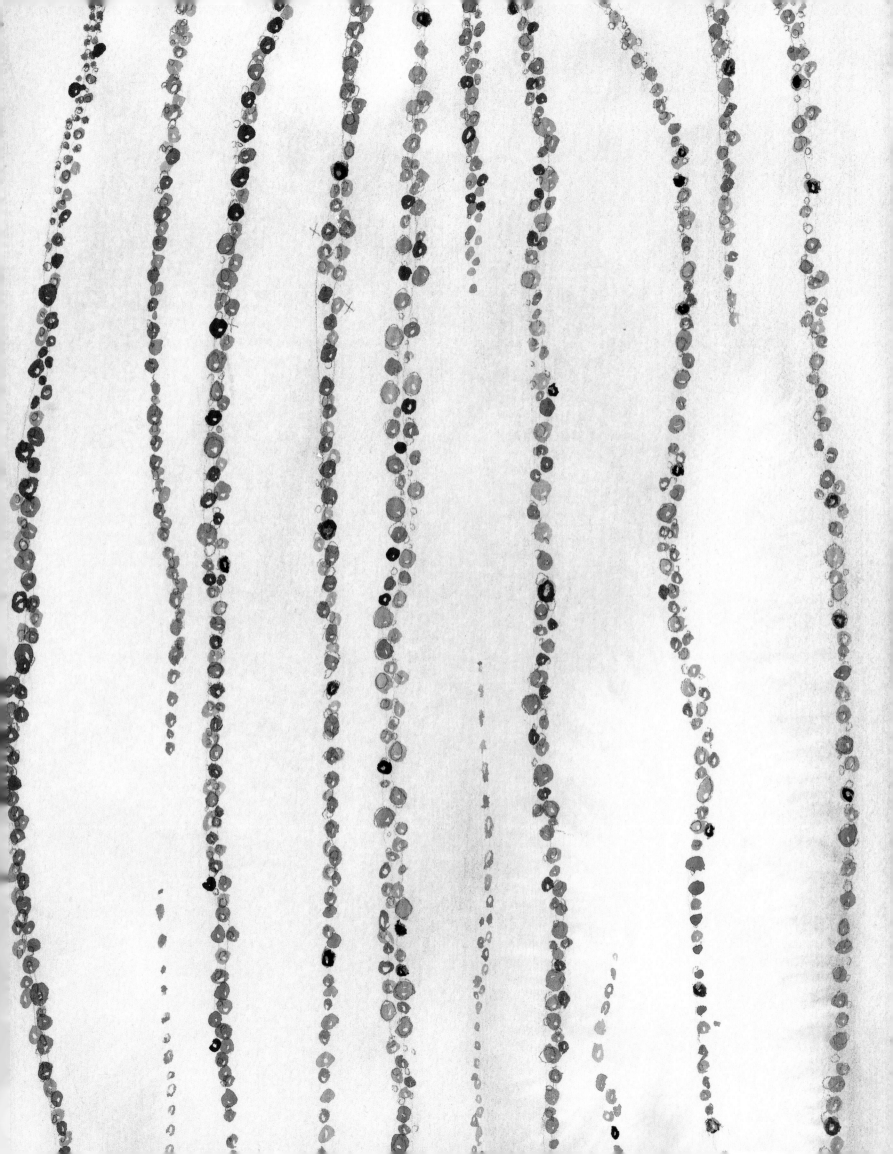

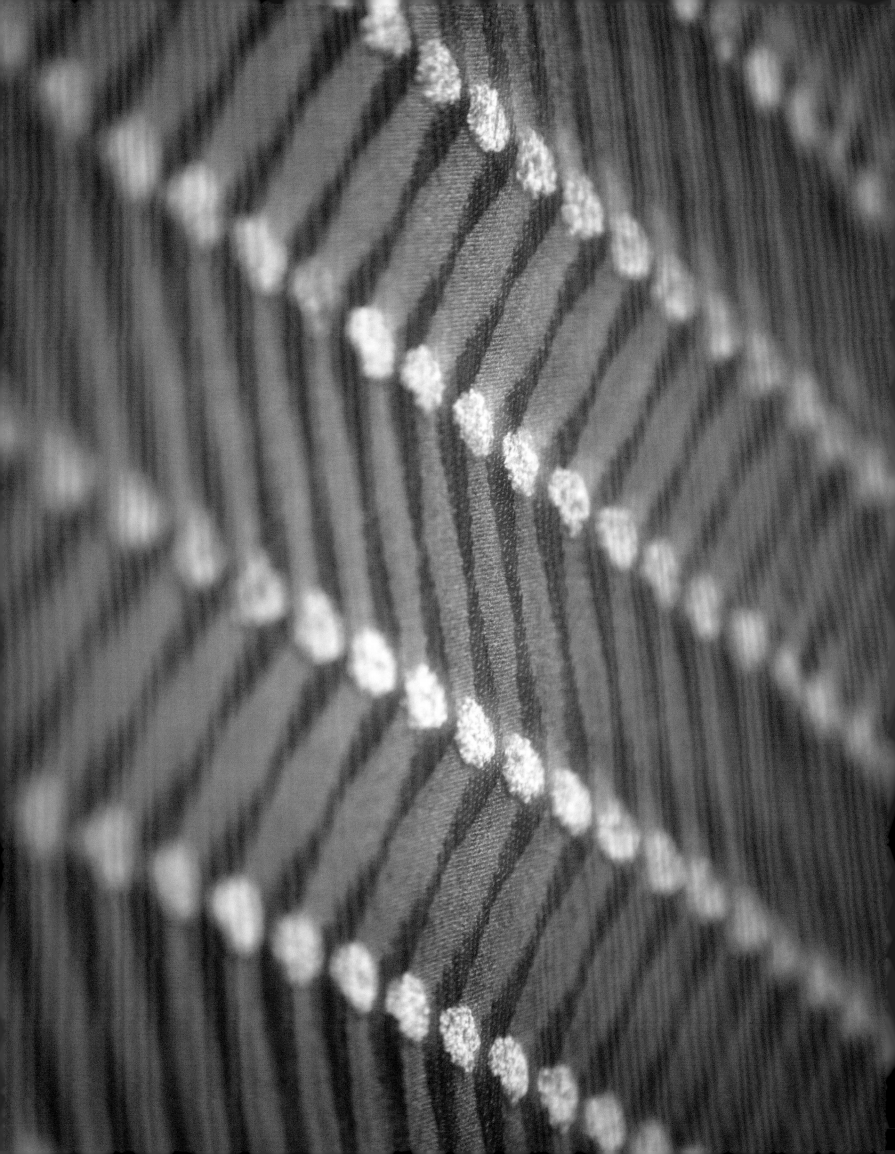

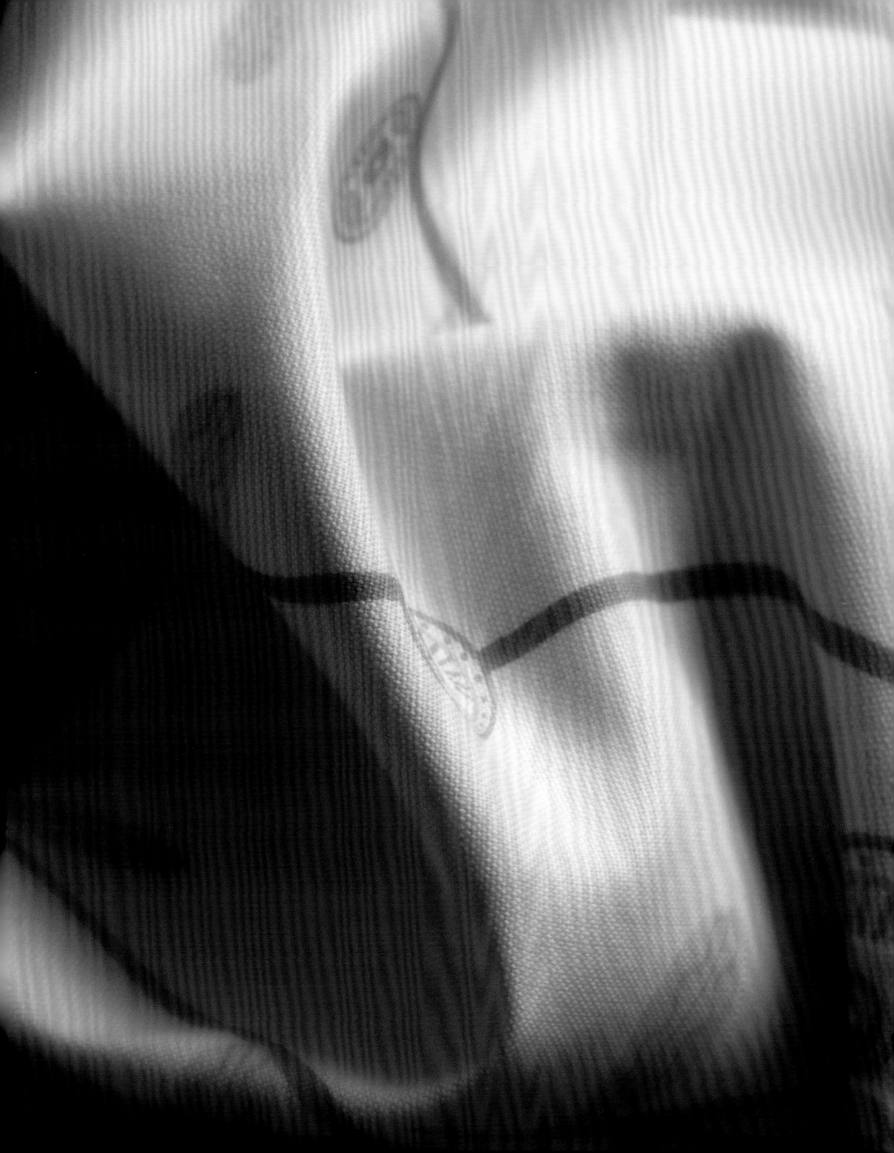

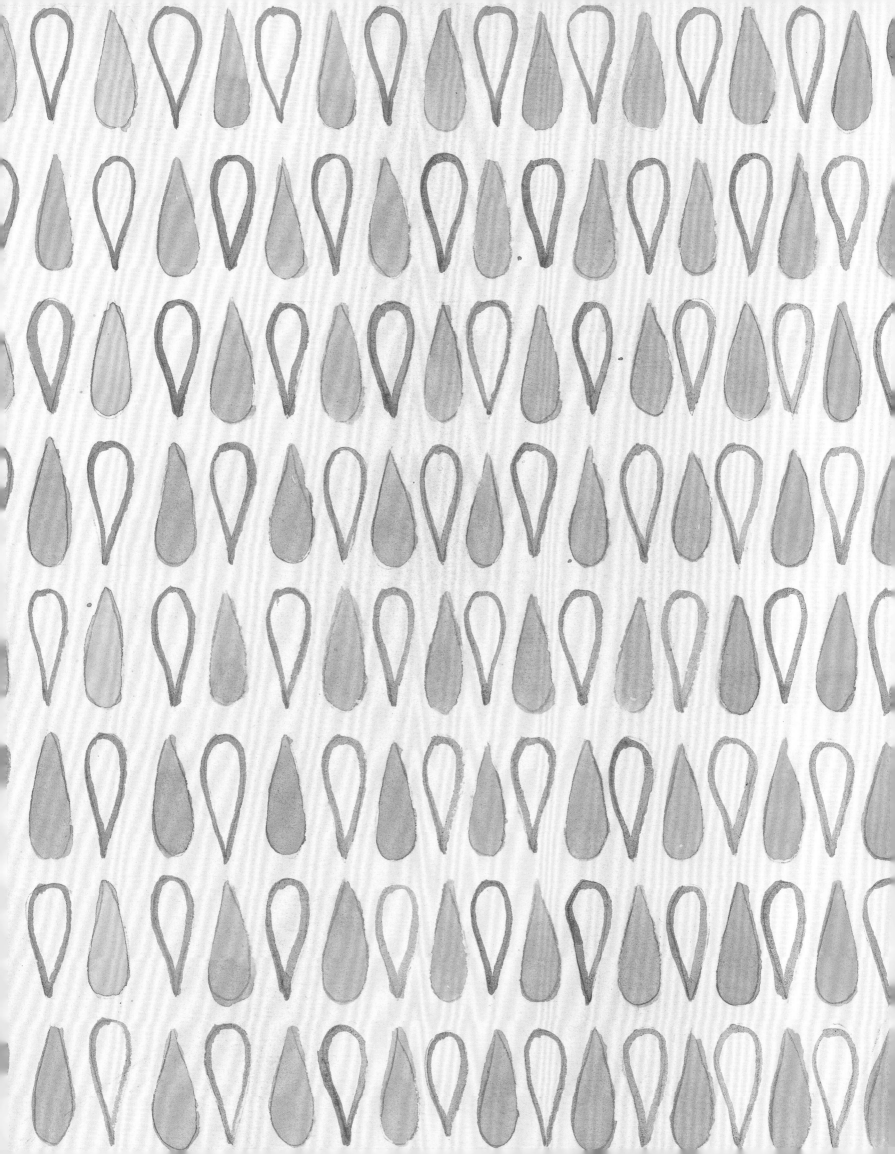

MEMORY

Our inspirations are never direct. They come from multilayered places, from something that is embedded in the mind and remembered in such a way that it becomes one's own. For example, the geometry in the rug on the previous pages is part of the alphabet that I started out with and that has stayed with me. Without such an alphabet, a personal style cannot develop or improve. I don't really know where this design came from, but I know it is essential to my aesthetic. A basic shape is to a design what a letter is to a poem. The starting point could be a childhood or adolescent memory, or even a very recent memory. It could be a mistake, a shape, or a work of art or vision you have always adored or even iconized. It could be anything. What matters is that the memory creates the shape, which becomes its own reference point and its own icon, without ever ceasing to be primitive and childlike, always remaining true to its origin. The imperfect rectangles here convey a sense of calm and belonging, almost as if one has always seen this design. Some designs, such as this one, are abstractions based on specific rhythms that come from deep memories. These memories start early in life. Their exact source usually remains elusive, but they progressively take shape and become a part of yourself, eventually expressing themselves through your creations. The pattern can then be repeated, giving the fabric a rhythmic, musical continuity. This is how a successful design quietly imposes itself on all the senses: Its inner logic simply makes sense. It can surprise, but never shock. It is in this way that design differs from art. Art is admirable and connects to an absolute. Design, on the other hand, is instrumental, useful, not absolute; it can be more natural and, in a sense, friendlier.

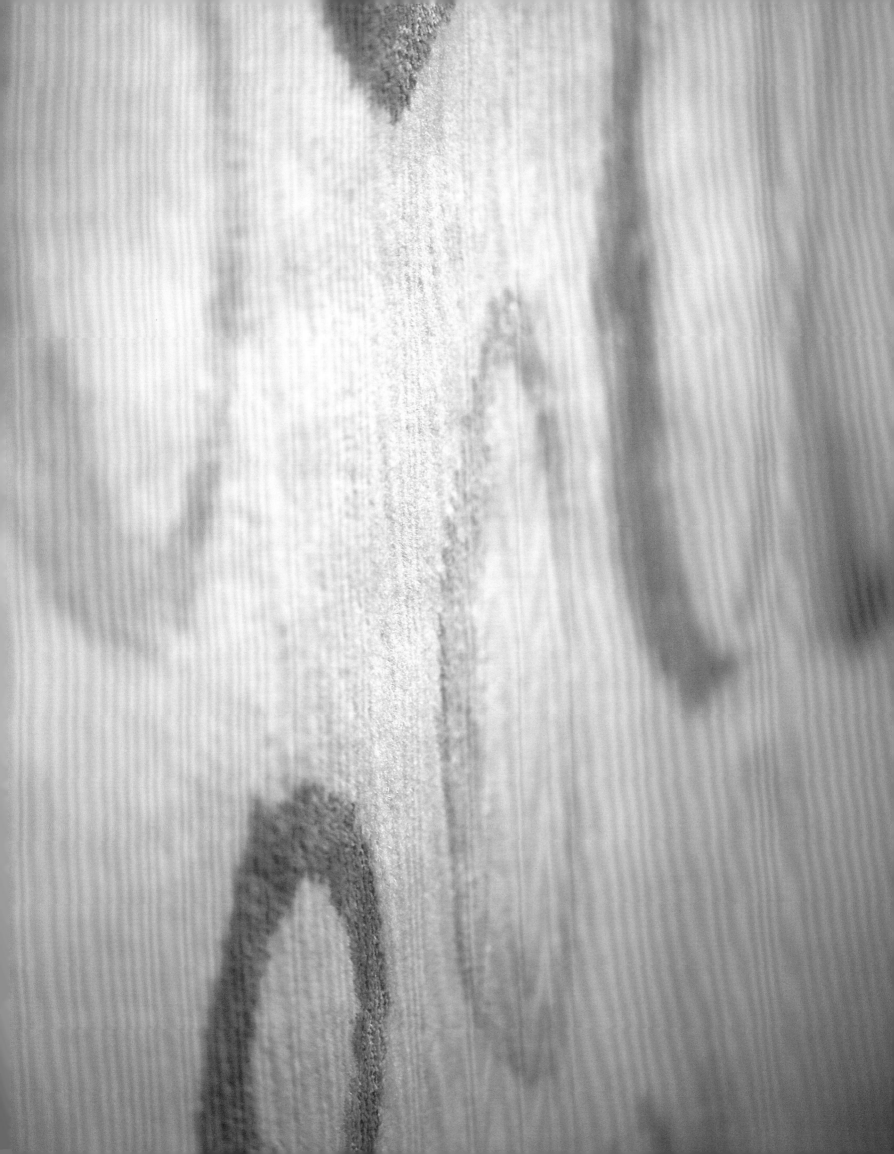

COMPLEMENTARIES

Combined blocks of different colors create a pattern. And juxtaposed, complementary colors—such as blue and orange, or pink and green—speak to each other as in a dialogue. Of course, sameness isn't necessarily monotonous in design. Sameness may constrain the eye, but it also creates a canvas onto which the viewer can create a whole world replete with tones and scales; it can even make the imagination soar. But opposites and complementary colors enhance each other, as Matisse, an artist whose vision I adore, knew very well. They guide us into a world of counterpoint and harmony, of musical pitch, and of balance between yin and yang. Blooming gardens are also composed of complementary colors that multiply like flowers; nature in springtime offers infinite variety and harmony. The juxtaposed green and pink fabrics on page 42 exhibit such harmonious complementariness. They are very feminine, delicate colors that recall the flowery, fragrant blooming of springtime. In my house on page 43, I juxtaposed a pink watercolor portrait of myself by Marina Karella—a feminine, almost sweet image, placed on a side table that is the first piece of furniture I ever bought in a flea market—with the nearby hard, metal staircase designed by Tom Dixon—starkly masculine, architectural and graphic. These are not contrasts but complements exhibiting a perfect balance between masculinity and femininity, just as pink and green are complementary colors. I like to encourage such conversations, which create pleasant visual tensions.

TEXTURE

When combined, textures can speak to each other in a very unexpected way. Take a luxuriously ethereal, soft, and feminine chiffon, such as on page 48, and juxtapose it with the picture of moss on the steps. The conversation between the two is wonderful and potentially very rich. I was inspired by the myriad greens of the moss to create a palette that is crucial to the look of the chiffon: the dominant yellow, the lines, blues, and turquoise all happily recreated in this interior shot. Each one has its own life, goes in a completely different direction, and does opposing things while feeding the other. The textures speak to each other: The moss is soft and humid, and it simply, even superficially, evokes a green watercolor that becomes a fabric whose own softness is emblematic of springtime. Using my own vocabulary, the softness of the moss is retranslated onto the delicate chiffon. But this translation isn't thought out or intellectual. Inspiration can come from many places—from a mood, or way of life, or a memory—but sometimes it is straightforwardly visual, as in the moss picture. Sometimes an image strikes us because of its purity—not because it is beautiful, but because it creates a new dynamic within our senses, shaking up our usual mode of perception and making us see something new, or anew.

MULTIPLICITY

Interiors should trigger curiosity and lead the eye to wander from corner to corner, surface to surface, shape to shape, and be open to the space in all its multiplicity. The path of the image on the previous page does this, indicating its own direction, as if exploring itself. This openness, this sense that any point in the room is the beginning of another visual path, can be created through a combination of details and colors that will keep the viewer interested. Patterns and combinations of patterns achieve this effect. The repetitive nature of the pattern in the warm, hand-stitched rug in this sitting room on the previous pages belies a multitude of possibilities. It is shaped of intertwined, half-finished hearts on a dark blue ground and is layered in such a way that it gives the overall effect of depth. Other patterns in this room work well here either because their alphabet evokes the rug or because their colors complement it. On the other hand, a detail or accent may work precisely because it clashes with other patterns. Different textures, colors, and sizes in patterns create a little story in which one can feel at home. When juxtaposing a variety of patterns or textures, as I do here, a conversation is created; you can choose a theme and then throw in a completely different note. This is how the patterns in an interior reflect a whole way of life, by echoing a way of dressing or conversing with others in the room.

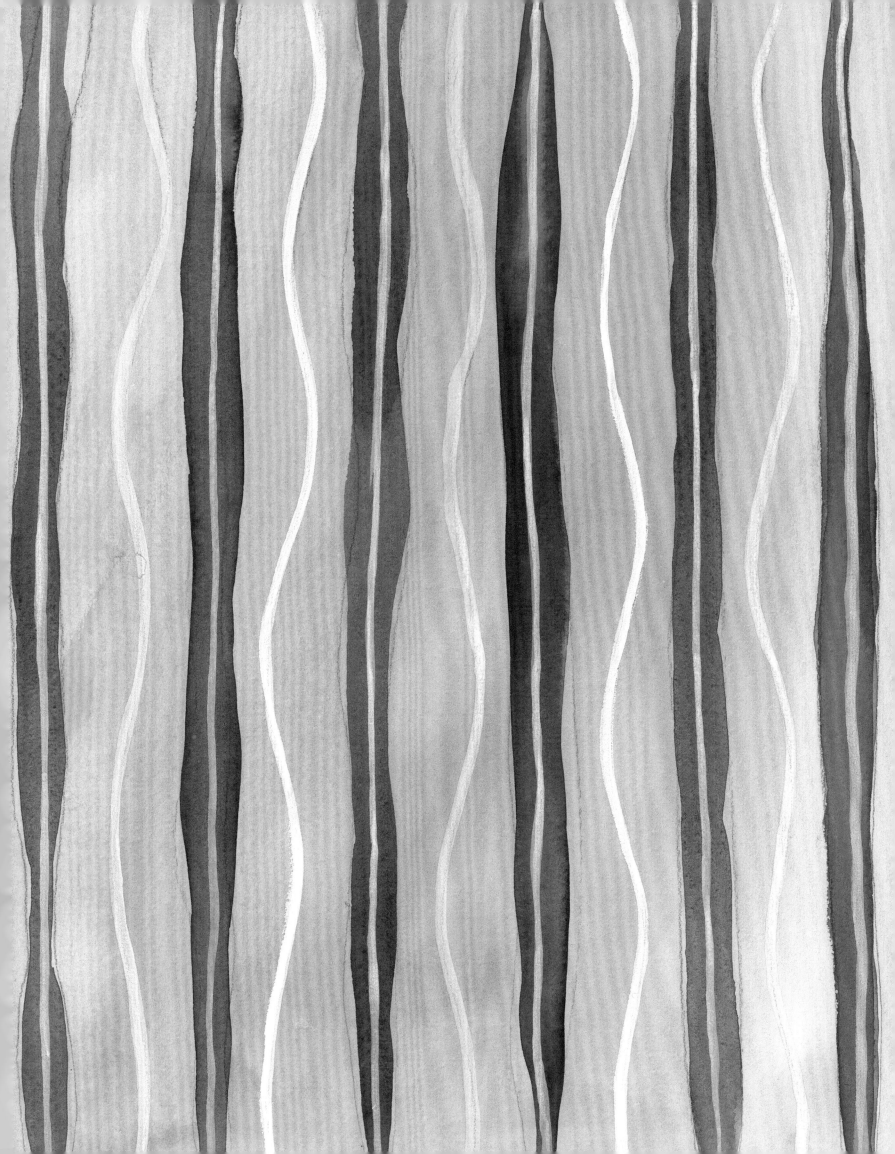

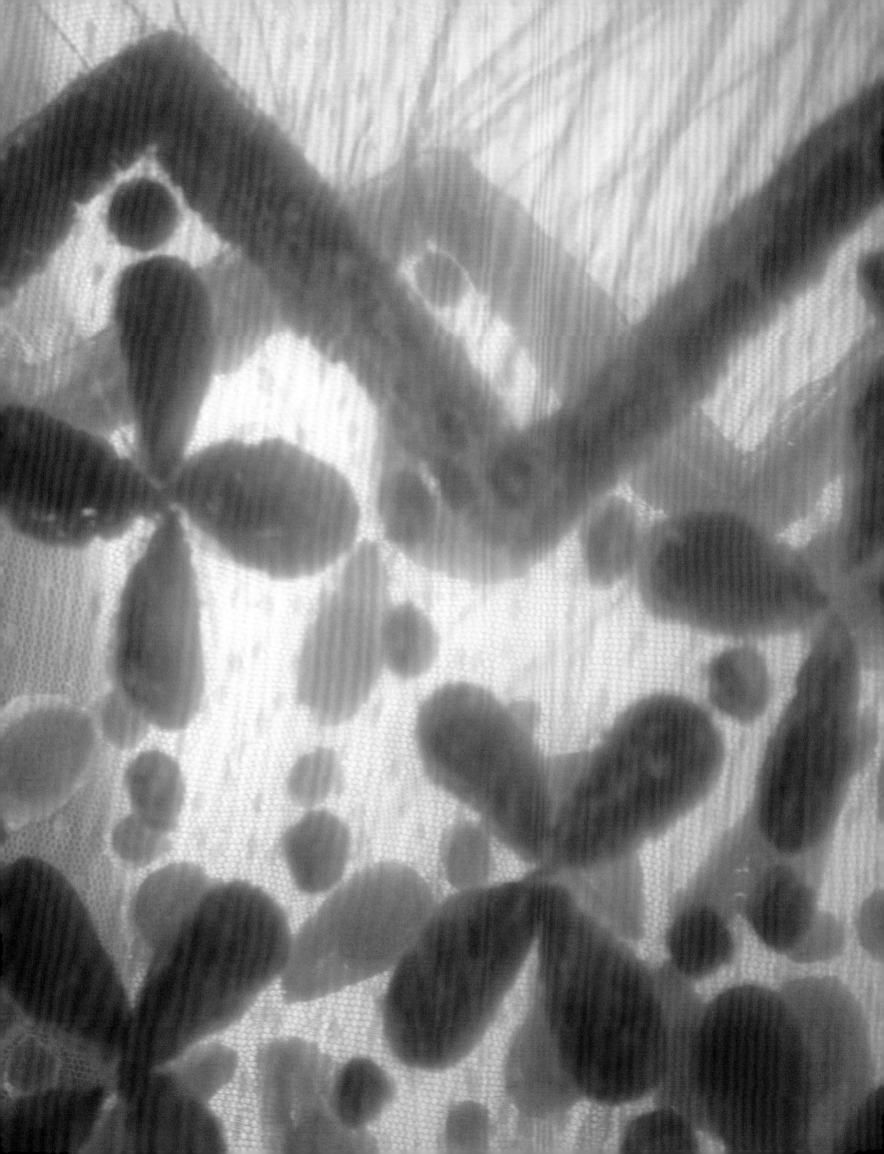

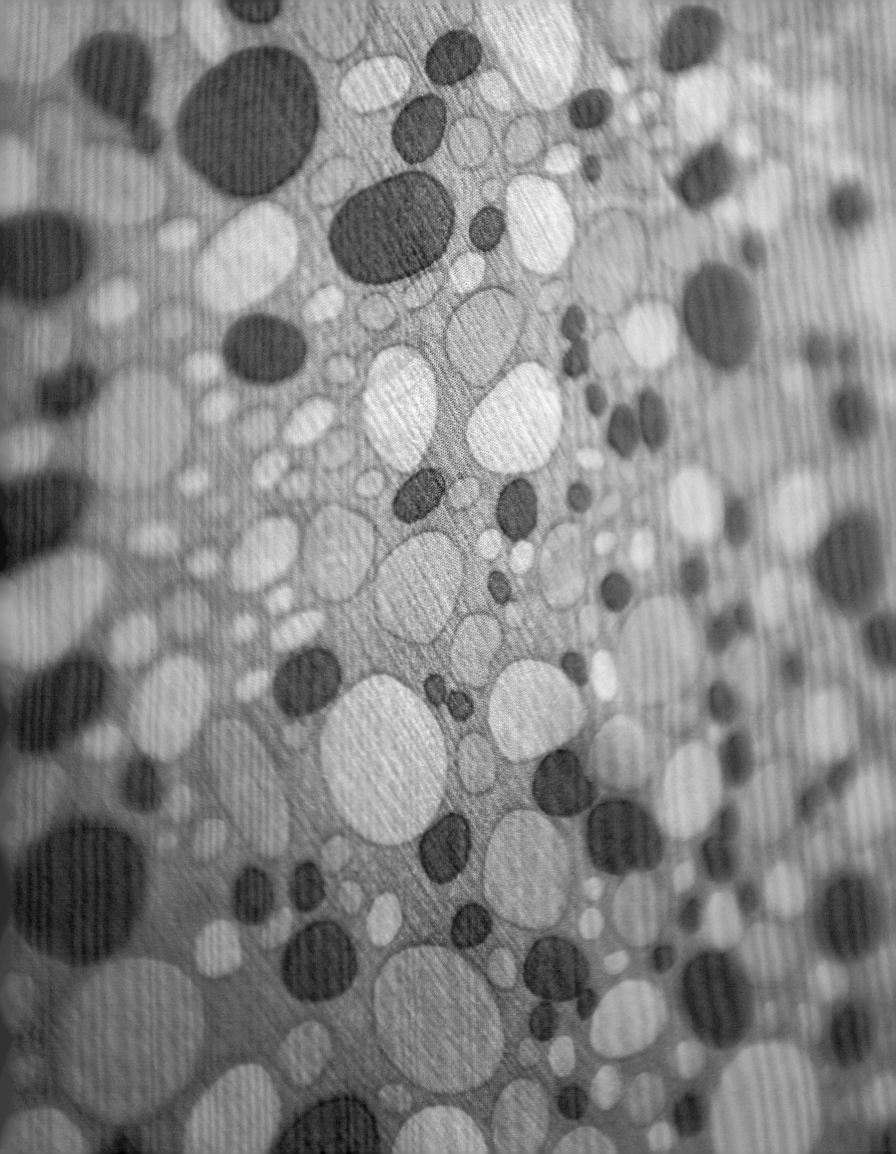

WATER

Spring pervades the patterns on the previous two pages, with water a key element of springtime. But one experiences water in a variety of ways in the spring. In one pattern, we are underwater, trying to get to the light; in another, we are striving to look down into water via a collection of drops that have left their mark on the surface of a fresh pond filled with greens and lilies. With one, you feel a light and feminine spring reflected in the translucent, embroidered silk, while the other is a more masculine spring as conveyed by the cotton fabric and the green and blue colors. In both, the palettes are beautiful and powerful, the spectrum is similar, and both are suggestive of harmony, which is what one wishes for in springtime. I like the conversation between these two fabrics, which are both born of nature and suggestive of water patterns. The textures are sensual yet fresh, in a way that is true to the season. The designs are at once abstract and suggestive of nature in an essential form. Both patterns are soft and breezy. They shirk willful geometry and are not constructed in any way; there isn't any underlying grid or any rhythmic repetition. Instead, the designs have organically and effortlessly landed in the right place—a harmonious, fluid answer to geometry.

SUMMER

IS A
TIME OF
CELEBRATION.
IT EVOKES HEAT,
THE SOUNDS OF
THE SEA AND SURF,
FIELDS RESTING
IN THE SUN,
THE SMELLS OF
STRAW AND LAVENDER,
AND THE SONGS
OF CRICKETS.

The skin
is exposed to
the elements,
caressed by
the warming sun
and soothing
breezes.

All of nature has come to life, fully grown and self-assured; the senses celebrate it, while a delightful indolence expands one's perception of time and space. This is a time of physical comfort and well-being.

The summer palette is a feast for the eyes. If spring is a watercolor, summer is a gouache. Its colors are saturated, rich, and celebratory; they explode with joy, entertaining the eye with oranges, purples, emerald green, turquoise, and lemon yellow. The days are long and the light can be blinding, so colors need to be stronger to be visible and not seem muted. The softer light of previous seasons requires softer colors that bear a somewhat abstract relation to the environment; now, in the summer, the colors in the fabrics are those of nature in summer—a ripe peach, the leaves in a tree, Tuscan hills, the burned fields, the yellow sun, and orange at dusk beneath a pink-streaked sky.

Water, always at the center of nature and transformed with each season, in summer evokes the turquoise sea and appears in summer fabrics in all its potency. In the spring, water is nurturing, but now in summer it is refreshing and a source of fun. Water in the summer is a gift for all the senses: Its salt tingles tongue and skin, its scents clear the head, its sounds flatter the ear, and its immensity calms the eye. The power of the sea relaxes. Movements are free, and so are the designs. They are larger, stretched; they flow freely, and their rhythm is slow like a Debussy piano piece. Some are graphic, but their repeats are broad and so they breathe, just as the summer air and sea cause us to breathe better and more slowly.

In the summertime, colors can freely clash; that is another aspect of summer's celebratory mood—the combinations can be jarring because of the saturated light. Think of Mexico, or India—bright, hot countries where deep pinks and oranges are often happily and satisfyingly paired. Use an equally deep yellow whose warmth embraces you in the summer. An intense palette accentuates the feeling of carefree ease engendered by the heat and enhances the beauty of places inside and outside. The oranges and yellows counterbalance the atmosphere of heat and sun, and are paired with complementary colors—strong blues, turquoise, and emerald green. All these are part of the natural landscape, and they dictate the design landscape; there is a perpetual conversation between nature and design.

Summer patterns are often like geometric doodles; they are graphic, but seem drawn by hand with wash and tempera. There is no transparency, just saturation. The designs epitomize heat while allowing room for some needed freshness. White, the summer equivalent of shade, tends to run along the breaks in the saturated color. Patterns are also playful because summer is a lighthearted season, nature's friendly gift. More time is spent outdoors, even late into the night's gentle air, refreshed by the saturated scents of vegetation. If spring can be compared to a Friday or Saturday morning when the whole of life is waiting to spawn and expectation is growing, then summer is Saturday night or Sunday, a time to be enjoyed because it will not last, because no expectation is possible beyond it, because autumn will announce itself after the first midsummer storm.

The designs always grow out of the same creative vocabulary; otherwise there would be no unity of style. But they morph with each season, through variations in colors and patterns, reflecting how our psychological states, not just our senses, change with each season. If spring is a time of timidity, then summer is a time of confidence. The open, confident assurance of summertime yields assertive colors, large patterns, and a vivid painterly touch that leaves behind the delicate watercolors of springtime and prepares us for the quiet thoughtfulness of autumn.

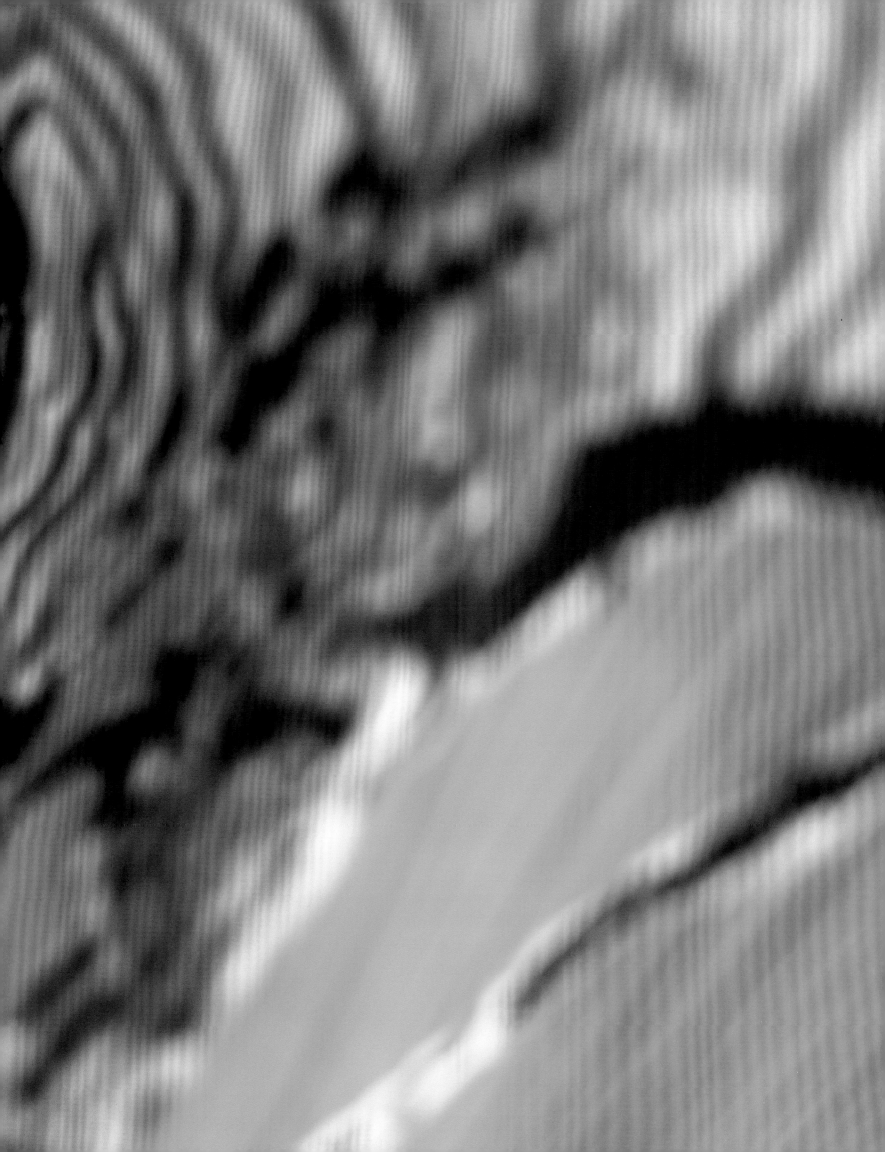

INDIA

For me, India is synonymous with the exotic, beautiful, spicy, and fragrant, with the utmost stimulation of all the senses. I was inspired by India the first time I went there, especially by the creativity displayed in the textiles, from those used in everyday life to the most ancient, precious pieces. The use of color is extraordinary and continues to influence my palette. Infinitely varied organic patterns are a constant everywhere, delighting the eye in the most unexpected ways. Certain places are evocative of seasons, and India, with its saturated light and colors, evokes summer. India's colors have an inspiring potency. There are no halftones, no fragile or subdued tonalities, just an endless lushness. And lushness is the key to summer designs. They may have a painterly feeling, shirking obvious geometry or straight lines for a more organic texture. The earth's geological strata make up the design on page 72, with its painterly alternation of strong colors and intense waves. Earthen, ochre colors are juxtaposed, literally grounding the eye. They are perfectly offset by, for example, the blue and yellow of a temple in Goa on page 73; I was inspired by the saturated reds surrounding it, by the orange, brown, and red colors of earth on a summer day. In India, the natural and the man-made are beautifully coherent; stone and earth are not jarring, and human constructions look natural. Design is present within nature, just as nature becomes present within my designs.

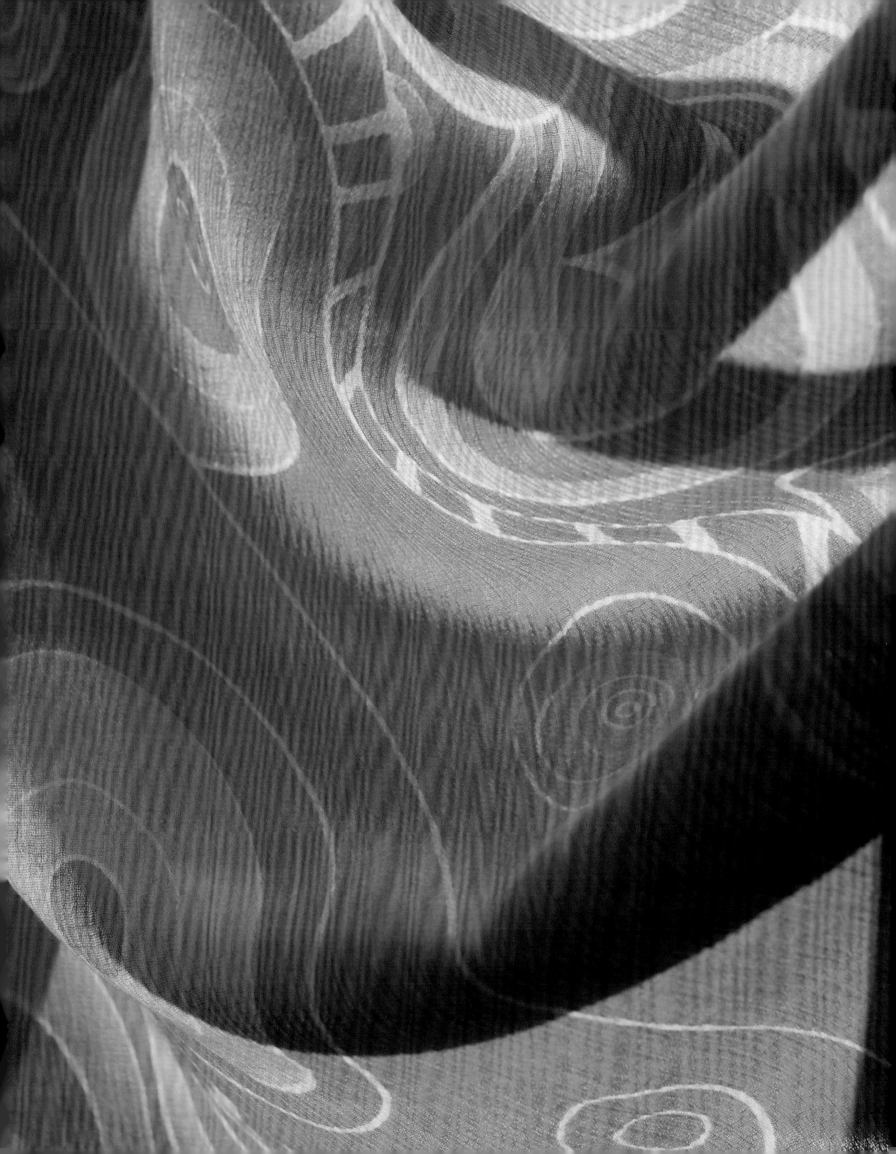

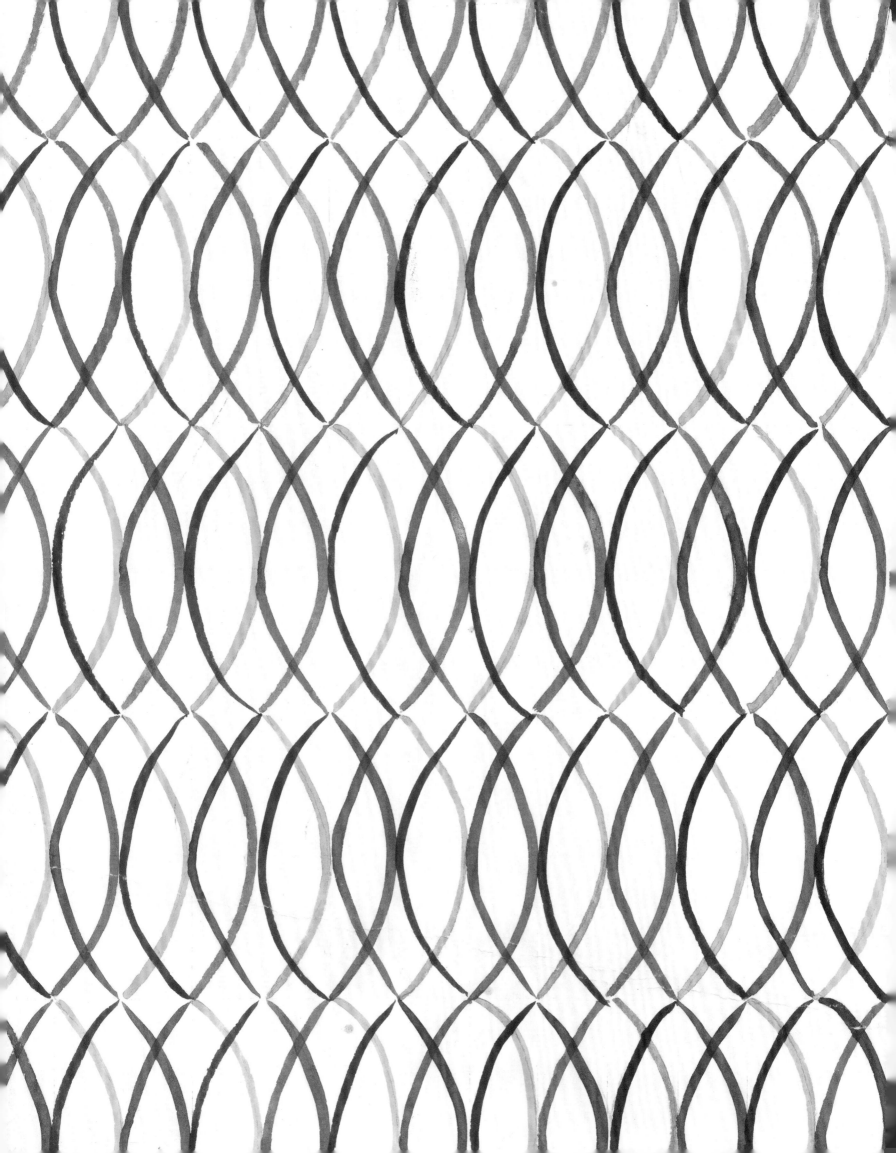

CONTRAST

In the heat of the summer, clear graphic elements converse with geometry. Summer allows the use of strong language and intricate yet simple designs. Summer is a time for decisive graphics and high contrasts. Yellow and black is a good combination that shows the highest possible chromatic contrast; The image on page 80 is inspired by the graphical composition I saw in a summerhouse in southern Italy shown on page 81. Black defines that design by setting off the saturated colors and emphasizing the lightness of the turquoise and white lines. The labyrinthine design in the fabric is softened with circles. A summer black is not sad; it is a noncolor background that allows strong colors to vibrate all the more. Here black reflects sunlight while itself absorbing light, and defining shapes, lines, and patterns. In the summer, black is cooling rather than cold, and it acts like a discreet backdrop that satisfies the eye by providing contrast, just as strong shadows emerge out of strong sunlight. Such contrasts can be stimulating, creating a theatrically visual effect. Chromatic opposites and the juxtaposition of black and white have a strong visual impact, imparting an interior space with the saturation of colors that prevail outside.

COMPOSITION

Composition is at the heart of design. It is a spatial as well as a chromatic matter that depends not only on line, but also on how colors bounce off each other. To compose is to engage in a balancing act with shapes and colors. Different states of mind emerge out of different color balances. Just as moods change with seasons, so can certain moods be evoked with a lot of light and a little darkness; the same design in different colors will evoke a different mood and look like a different design. The size and density of patterns also affects moods and the general effect of a design; the same design will have a very different visual impact depending on its scale. For instance, a repeat of a small leaf looks like a leaf, but on a very large scale, the same leaf becomes an abstract design. I like playing with these effects. Scale is also very important in interiors; the right scale will make the room coherent, livable, and pleasant. Groups of small objects can also have an impact on fabrics, changing the way in which you see the patterns' scale. Composition and coloration together change the rhythm, message, feeling, and use of a fabric. A strong yellow carries summer inside; as it turns more golden, it conveys the preparation for the end of summer and the start of autumn.

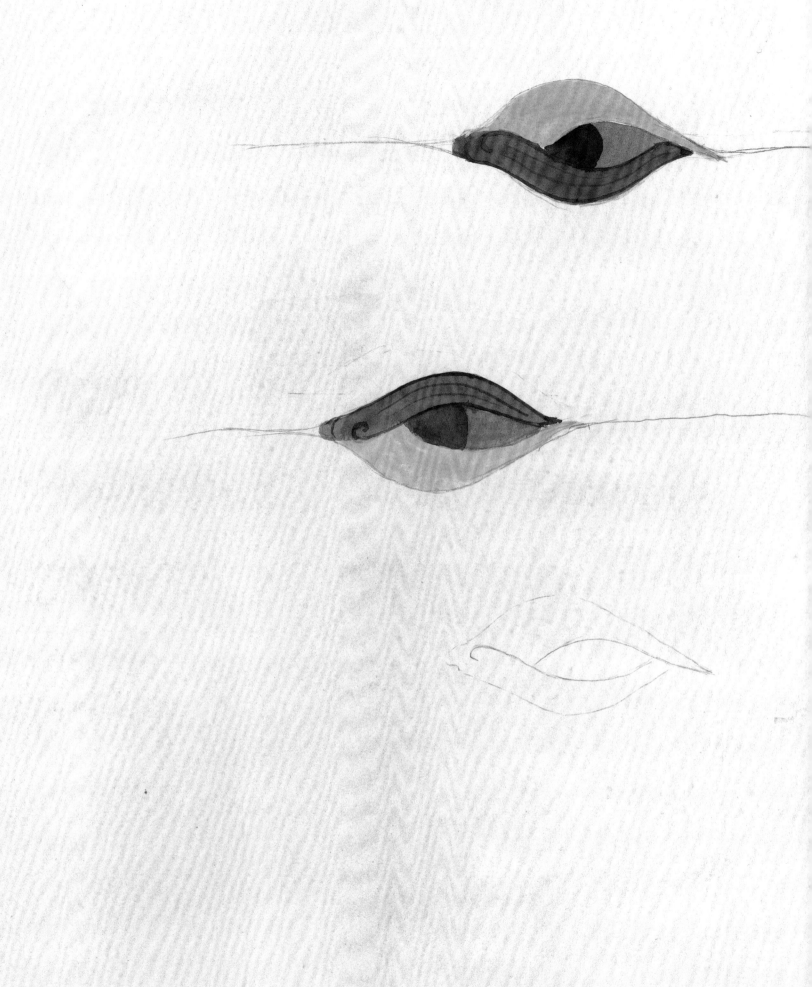

ENERGY

Summer is about explosions, fireworks, and joy bursting out everywhere. Just as spring needs to cultivate and preserve new energies, so summer is a time when energy explodes and when nature gives its all. We live outside, deeply connected to nature, and leave summer with sensuous memories—of the smell of honey and peaches, of the sound of wasps and bees busy gathering nectar. When I was a child, the three months of summer holiday were long and lazy, but they were also the most creative months, during which we had to find things to do, paint, draw, or invent new games. Summer fabrics reflect that activity and energy, the joy of being alive. Dahlias, for instance, are the perfect summer flowers, and on page 94, they convey clean freshness and explosive energy. The crisp white refreshes and keeps the heat away; white is light and summer is a time when you use light. Shadows grow out of light, giving way to geometric designs, and because shadows are strong and color-ful in the summer, I use unrelated colors to produce more fireworks and more explosions of joy.

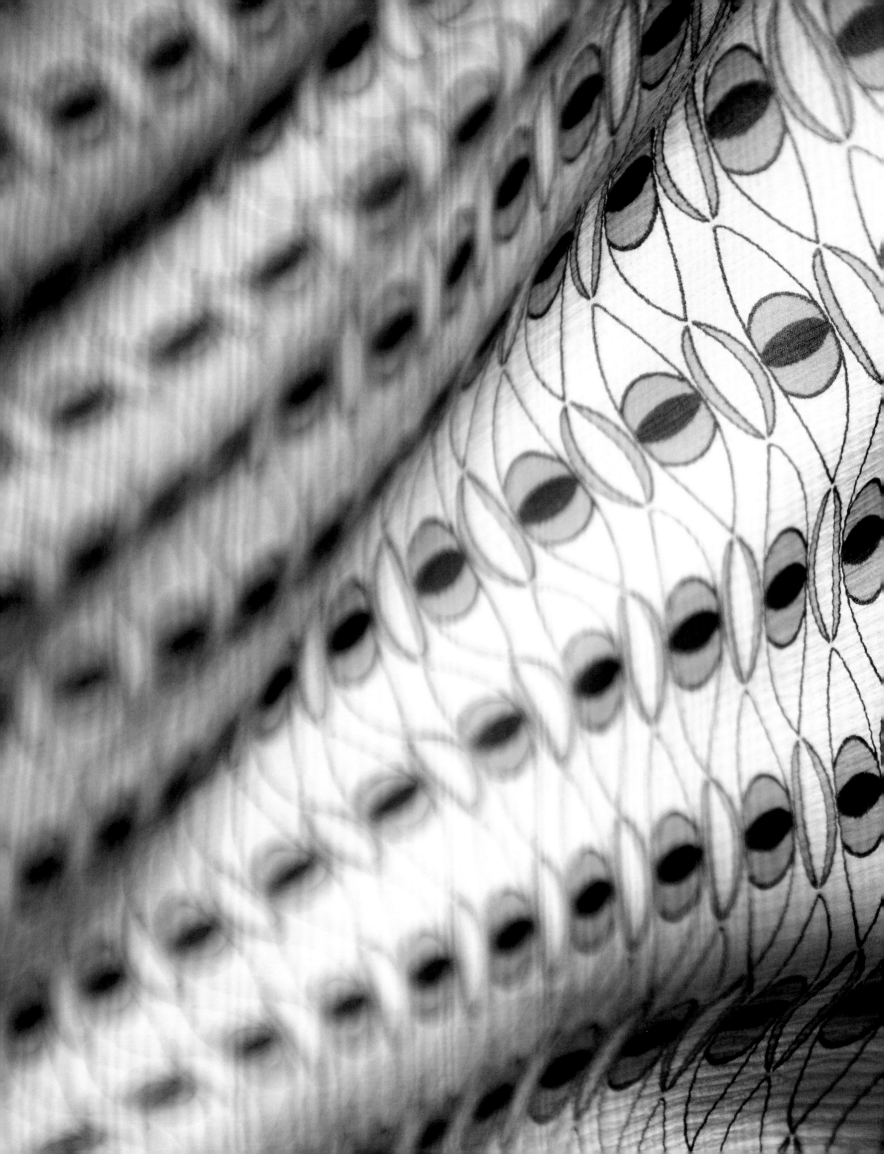

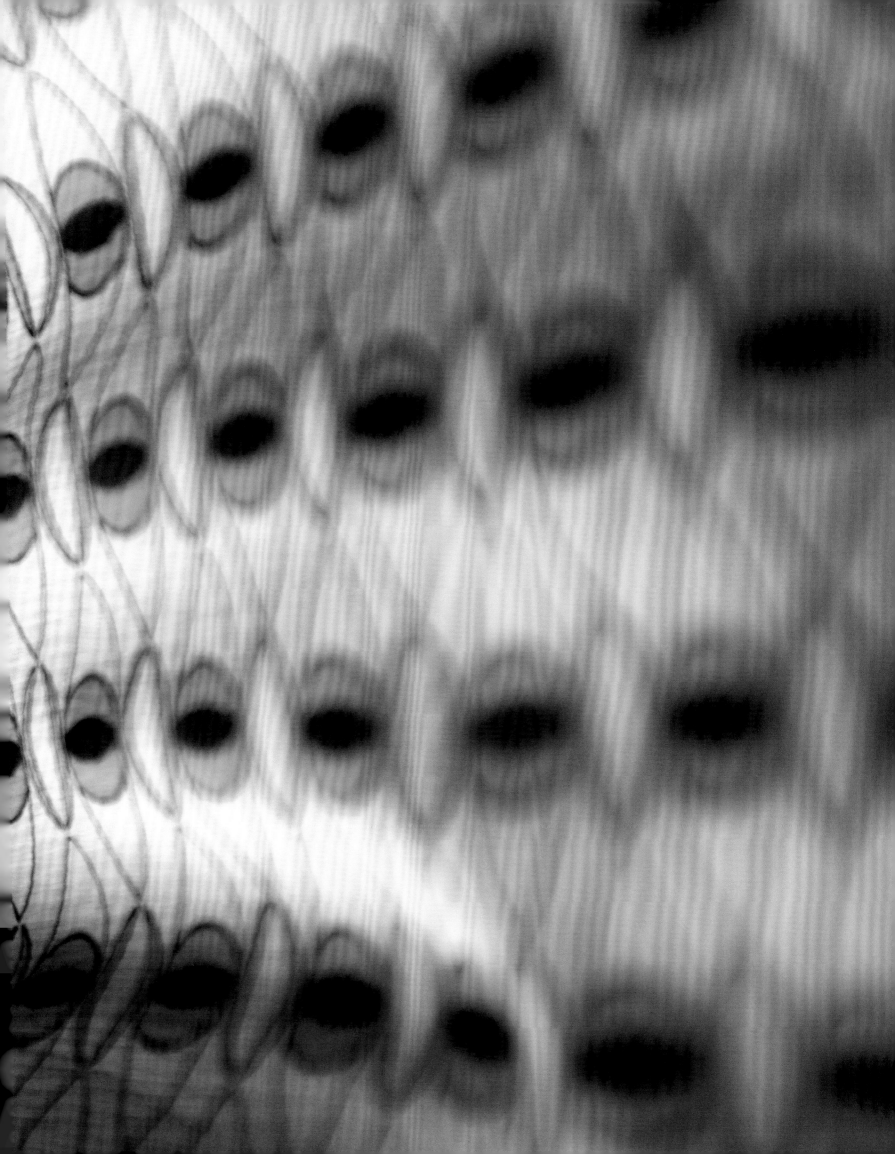

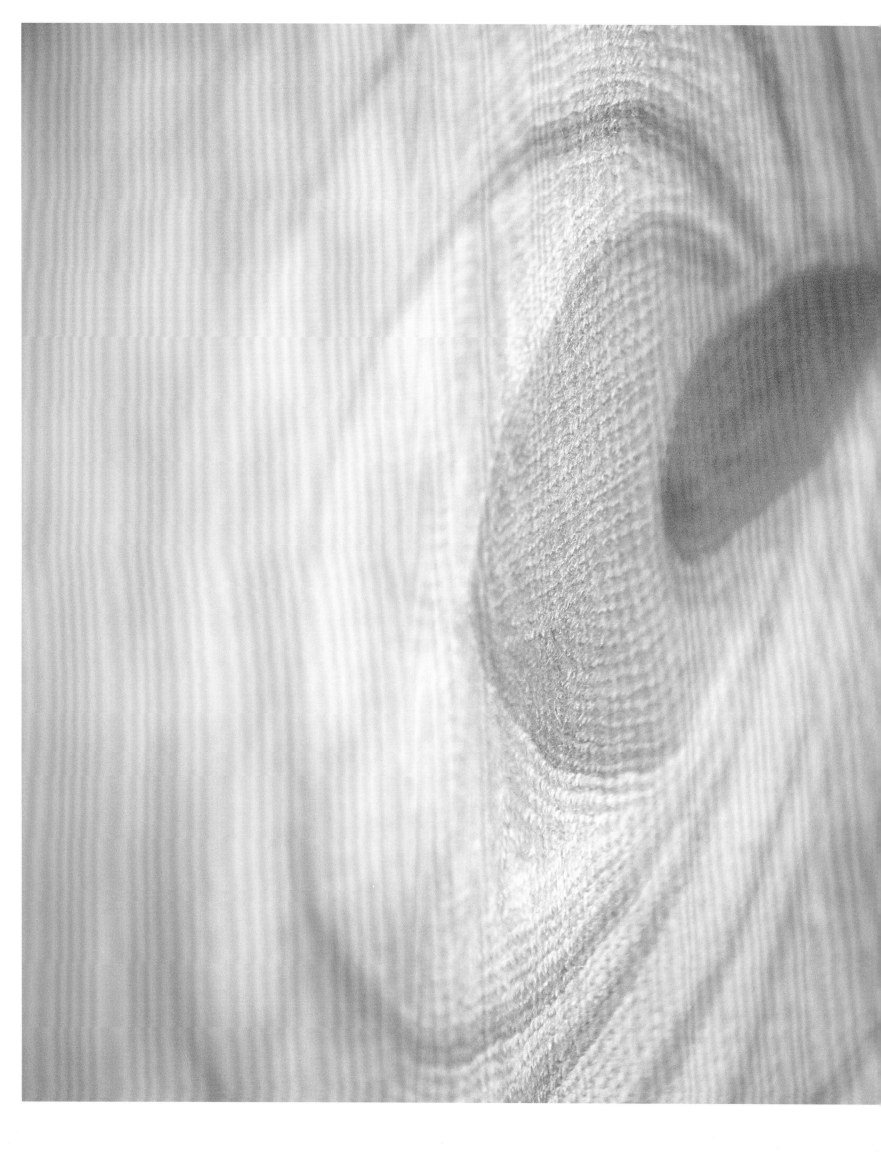

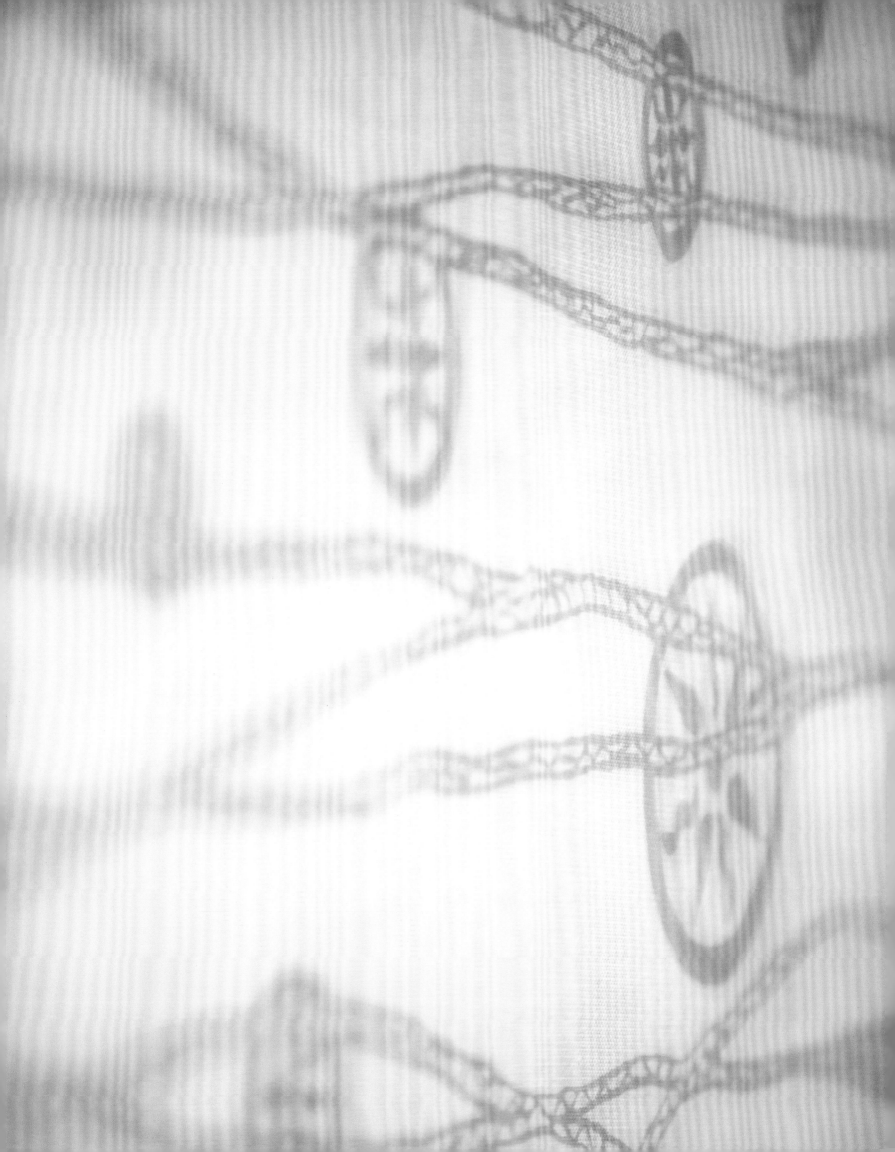

ECLECTICISM

I like to pair clashing colors or themes and designs that at first seem unrelated. Juxtapositions of this sort start in the wild and then are developed in gardens. In one such Tuscan garden on page 113, a rose and a tomato have been planted and grow next to each other. Roses are synonymous with beauty, and fruit with nourishment. Generally, you would not think of planting the two together. Yet I think this unconventional notion of what can happen in a garden results in natural beauty. It is a very Italian, straightforward eclecticism, a freedom from convention that satisfies the eye and all the senses. Purism isn't necessary. Different species can mix; you don't need to create a rose garden here and a row of tomato plants there. Vision, smell, and taste combine in one place, in one experience where sensations bounce off each other. Roses are delicate and fragrant; tomatoes are delicious, sweet, juicy, and incarnate the promise of summer at its most delightful and sensuous. Summer is precisely about this fulfillment, and its fabrics translate and transmit the enjoyment of all the senses.

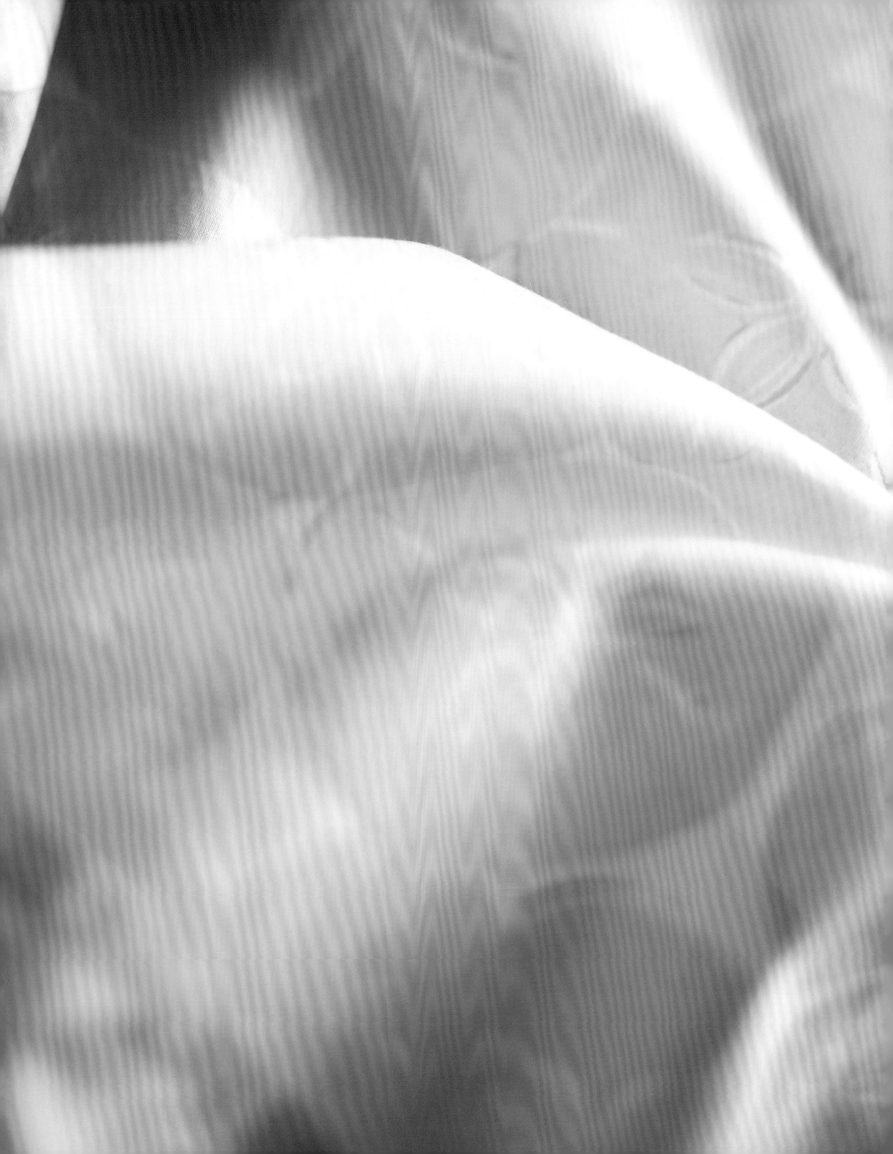

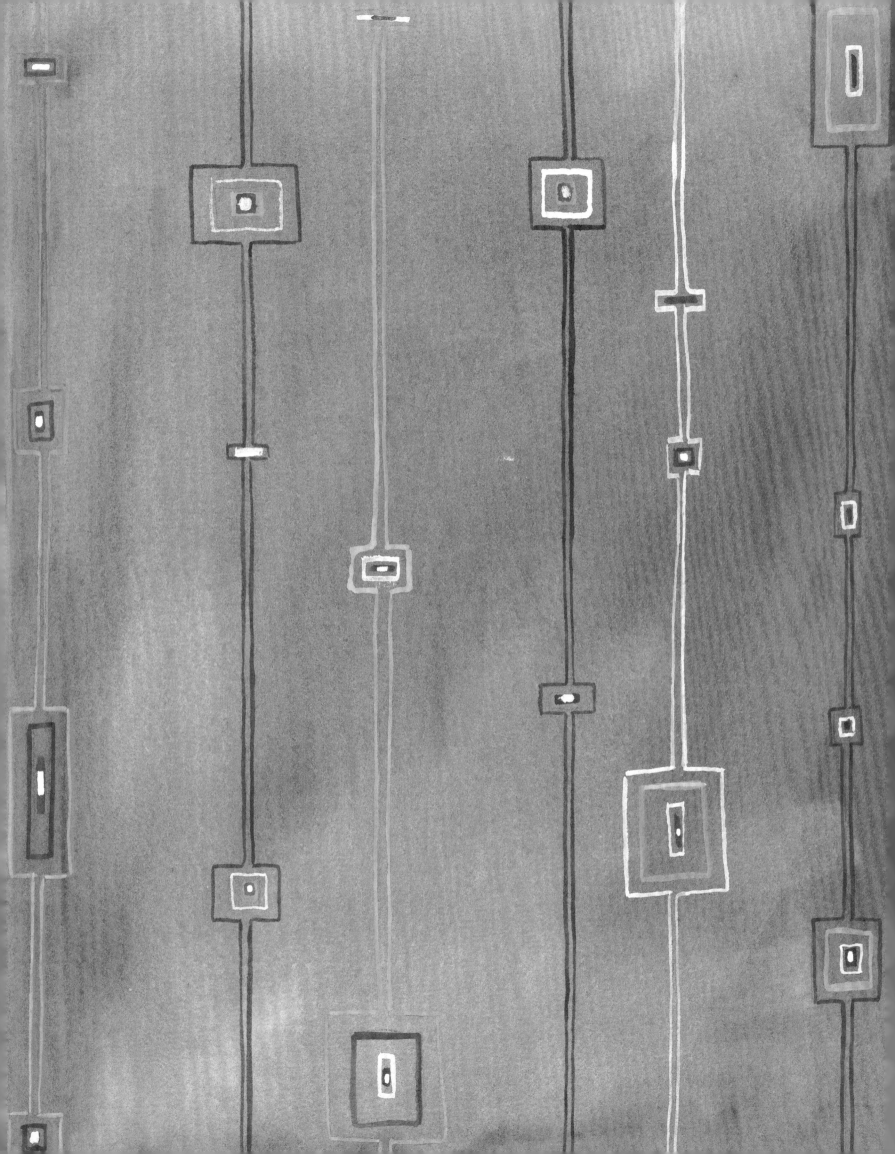

AUTUMN

IS A TIME
FOR WARMTH,
WHEN A SUBDUED
RICHNESS TAKES
THE PLACE OF
THE LIGHT AIR
AND EXPLOSIVE
COLORS OF
SUMMER, AND
WHEN ONE WANTS
TO BE EMBRACED
BY SOFTNESS.

If spring was
a watercolor
and summer
a gouache,
then autumn is
an oil painting,
its atmosphere
thick with
scents and
humidity.

Fabrics are warm now and colors are soothing. It is the season when grapes are harvested for wine; its eponymous hues are emblematic of autumn, like the warm touch of velvet.

Autumn represents the conclusion of the day or late afternoon. It marks the end of lightness and long days, the beginning of the working calendar after the long summer break, and a time of seriousness when one spends more time indoors. The light outside is crisp, golden, and rich in deep hues. Almost like magic, colors mutate from the azure, turquoise, and greens of summer to ochre, sienna, and red. The autumn colors that find their way into fabrics are thick, opaque, and multilayered like a Cézanne painting. I use a variegated, saturated palette, where warm reds, oranges, and midnight blues evoke warmth and encourage you to stay indoors. When it is dark outside on an autumn evening, a well-lit room needs these warm colors reminiscent of the scent of grilled chestnuts, burned leaves, gentle rain, damp woods, and fireplaces. The warm texture of velvet envelops and creates an atmosphere of elegance and softness that mirrors the textures of autumn and suggests the tastes of the harvest.

Autumn leaves are no longer the lush, green breath of trees; they twirl in the wind, shift from frank color to blushing ochre, and disconnect from the trees' life-giving sap. They are a choreographed, chromatic kaleidoscope of free-floating apparitions that embody the cycle of life and death, a perfect organic pattern that becomes central to my design alphabet. Nature is still yielding its harvests and fruit, and one can still render their shapes into a pattern, yet autumn marks the end of nature's cycle, and so this is also the time when abstraction begins to take over.

The resulting patterns are more graphic than before. They display contrasts without using clean or primary colors. Subdued tones predominate, while lines clearly direct the eye, like a river. Nature does not stop in autumn, a season akin to a gently flowing river with hidden currents. Nothing is still; the weather changes from Indian summer to days of cold rain and wind. Accordingly, the designs are also less predictable than in other seasons, less tonal, at times even jarring. Their lines are vibrant, at once alive and utterly abstract. The theme of drops, which has always been part of my vocabulary, recurs in autumn, too, but abstracted, repeated, and strongly graphical.

Patterns are the intellectual elaboration of natural elements; the conversation between the observation of nature and the abstraction of it, so central to my creative process, is particularly intense in this season of transformations. The autumnal to-and-fro between the organic and the graphic gives birth to designs that, although they begin in nature, now depart from it. They organically grow into a source of sensual pleasure, much like decomposed leaves feed the soil from which new plants will grow in the spring, after the winter frost.

ABSTRACTION

Nature can be used at once in a literal and an abstract way. A natural detail can become so abstracted that it no longer bears a direct relationship to its model; it becomes an essence, an idea. For instance, the bamboo plant that I used as a source of inspiration for the rug on the previous pages is at once present to and hidden from the eye within the design. The colors are those of a bamboo plant, but the design is an abstraction. It is only through the use of colors that the design is able to retain a natural look; the pattern of this vividly geometric design is an abstraction. Yet an abstraction, like a landscape, can condition a mood. Both instinct and intellect are at play, with the success of a design dependent on fostering a harmony between the two. The patterns of the pillows on page 133 are also abstractions, suggestive of a natural order with an autumnal feel; one begins as a sunburst and the other as an animal shedding its skin. In this case, the design is more literal than the colors, which mutate in the way that leaves change their colors in the autumn, thus turning these patterns into abstractions.

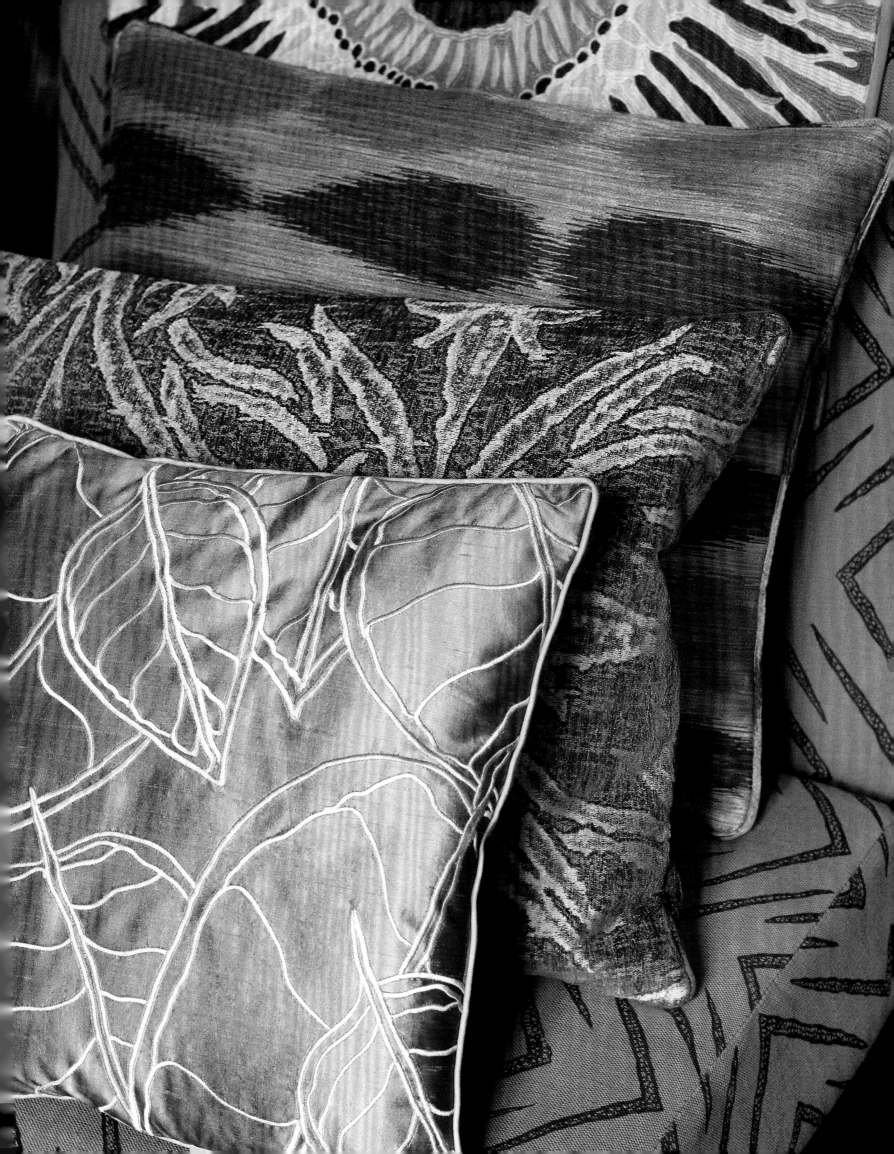

PAINTING

Autumn is about the layering of sensuous and thick textures, like an oil painting. The watercolor transparency of springtime and the yearning for freshness in summer evolve into a three-dimensional texture that I like to enhance. In autumn, there is a need to be enveloped by textiles like cushions on the previous page, whose layers encourage you to slow down your thoughts and activities. These layers complement each other, creating a lush ensemble in purples and dirty pinks that suggest the colors of a vineyard. The mood conjures the smells and tastes of autumn that cause the senses to relax into the warmth of soft textures, such as woolen embroideries, heavy silks, and velvets. All these textures evoke a sense of richness, ripeness, and well-being. The quality of the design is that of a sensuous, warm, energetic, yet soft brushstroke.

MOVEMENT

A textile can be the beginning of a voyage of discovery—not just of the world, but simply of the home one lives in. The pattern on page 140, for instance, covers a whole staircase. With its dirty blue and wine colors, all on a backdrop of a gray autumn sky, it leads the viewer up and down the stairs. But this textile doesn't just decorate a much-used surface and well-traveled passageway; it also affects your mood, movements, and daily rhythm. That is because designs are essentially rhythmic. The ellipses in this design repeat themselves in a pattern that is like a musical theme. Indeed, to my mind, design, like painting, can be powerfully reminiscent of music; inversely, design and painting can inspire musical creation. Patterned form, rhythm, and counterpoint are all musical elements as well as elements of design. Movement, too, is central to music, and this image is a case where a design is profoundly musical, indicative of movement and also conducive to it. Like music, design involves all the senses, which are stimulated by the act of seeing. In this way, an autumn design will not only look autumnal, it will have an autumnal feel. And like music, design is evocative, not just indicative.

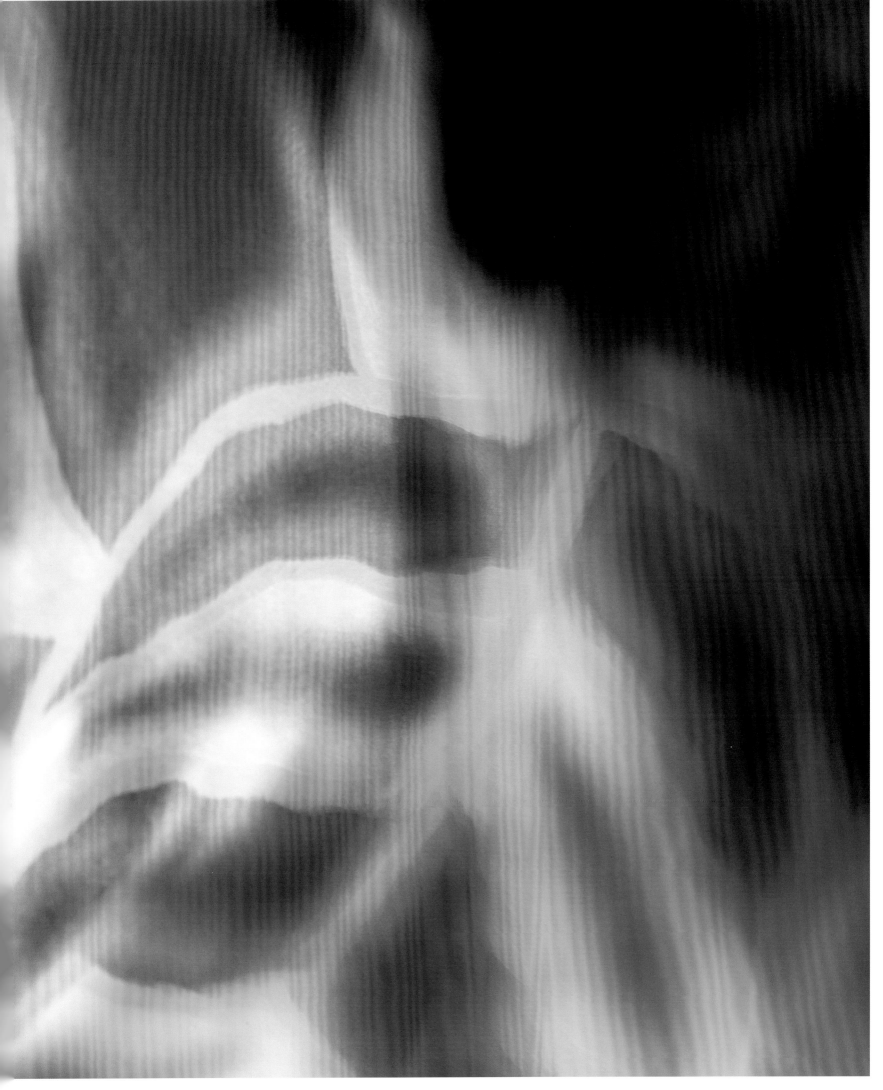

GEMS

I am quite aware that you can never improve upon natural colors, but by observing them, you can create beauty. Stones, of course, are not alive, yet their colors confer upon them a lifelike quality. This is how nature gives us a ready-made design. The room on the previous spread is an inspiring environment filled with stones and other objects, from fossils to feathers. It is a veritable cabinet of curiosities that I love to plunge into. Nature becomes an exhibit of sorts and a direction for design.

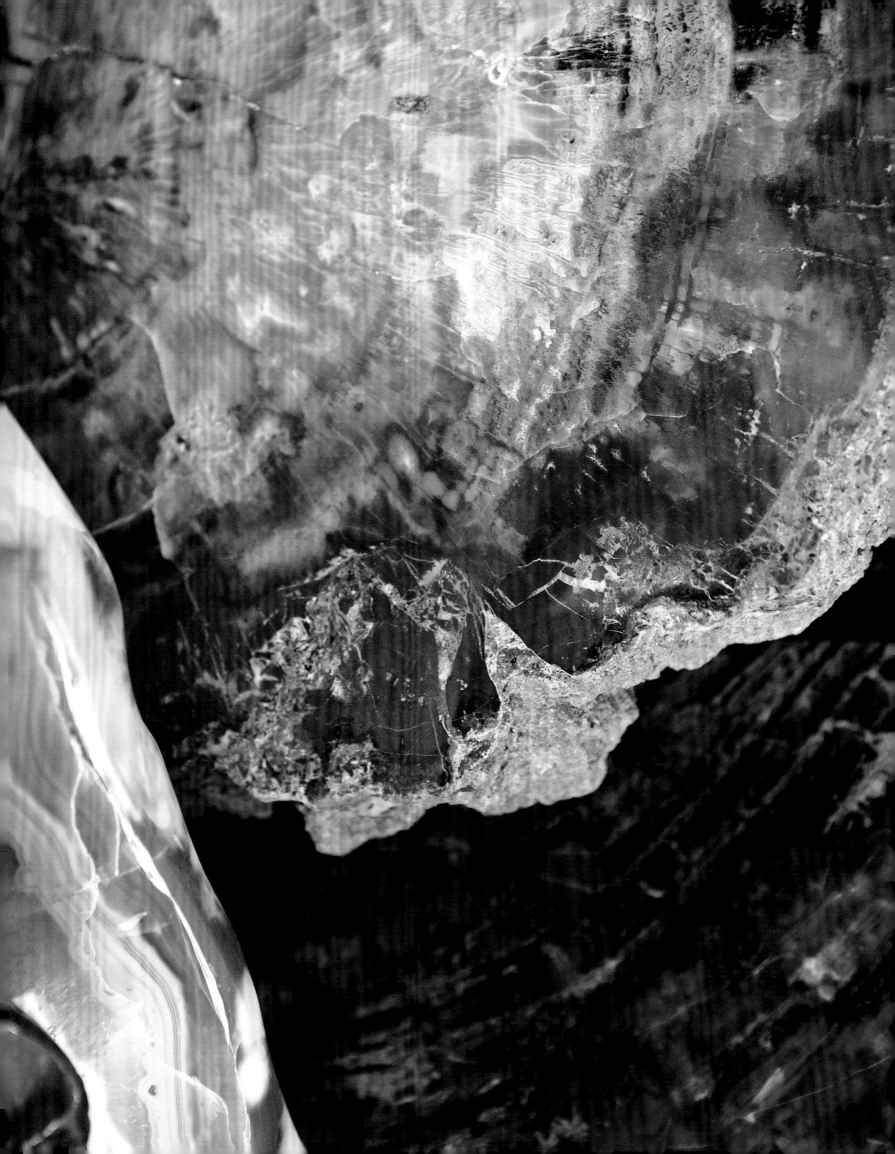

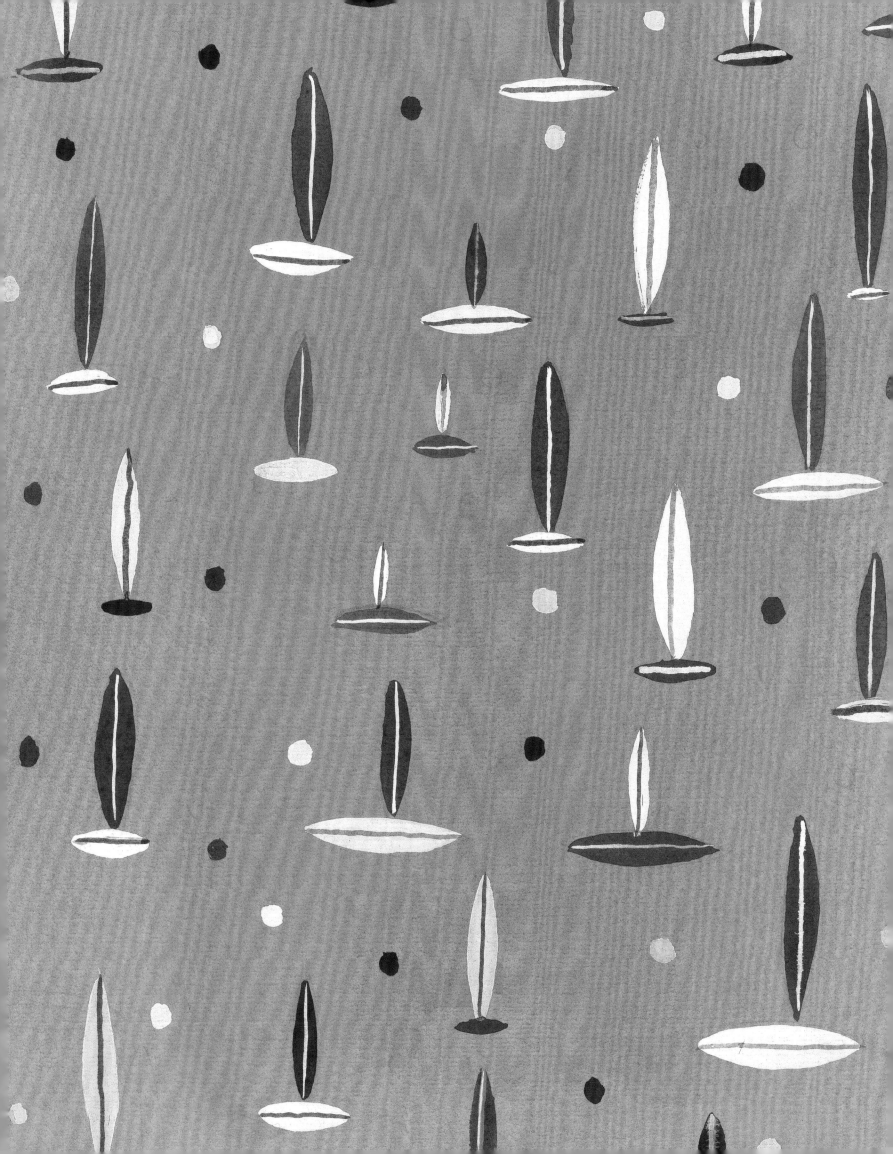

ELEMENTS

Nature's microcosms are an unending source of inspiration. They are a source for pairing, manipulating, and interpreting colors until a new, man-made element is created. Nature's elements make up the visual poems that are designs. Looking at nature as through a microscope can open up a world of images that belong to the world of nature but are also highly sophisticated. Much of my inspiration comes from such attention to natural form. The petrified tree on page 155 offers a kaleidoscope of colors; its very design is free, neither caged nor willed by the human mind. It offers a palette that is natural yet highly composed: ice reds and a touch of brown, strong elements that when translated to interiors perfectly describe the end of autumn. The fabric on page 154 has an entirely different palette, but its color values are similar to those of the tree. It is also reminiscent of a butterfly wing, another microcosm of extreme sophistication that is at once ordered and random. I am inspired both by nature's order and its disorder.

FRAGILITY

The petals of the datura flower on page 165, pungent like an amaryllis, die as soon as they are picked. I find that flower very inspiring. Although it is a summer flower, its fragility is emblematic of autumn, and, to me, the veins of its petals seem to create a map of the soul. It corresponds to a fabric that combines velvet and patchwork on page 164 and that tells a story of how the flower is impacted by natural elements. The flower and the fabric generate a sense of life in suspension, both autumnal and fragile. Each in their own way, they translate the feeling of the season. They summon the sense that life is nearly gone, but the memory of it is retained within the fabric's folds and within the golden colors of the sun at the end of a short day. Even when a fabric is thick, rich, and soft, as is this silk, it can still be associated with autumn's chill. Likewise, even a summer flower may be used as the starting point for encapsulating within threads the fragility and barely perceptible changes of autumn. An association between a natural object and a textile need not be literal. Autumn is not only represented inside a room by color and texture; its essence can also be made concrete through ideas. The fragile datura is such an idea.

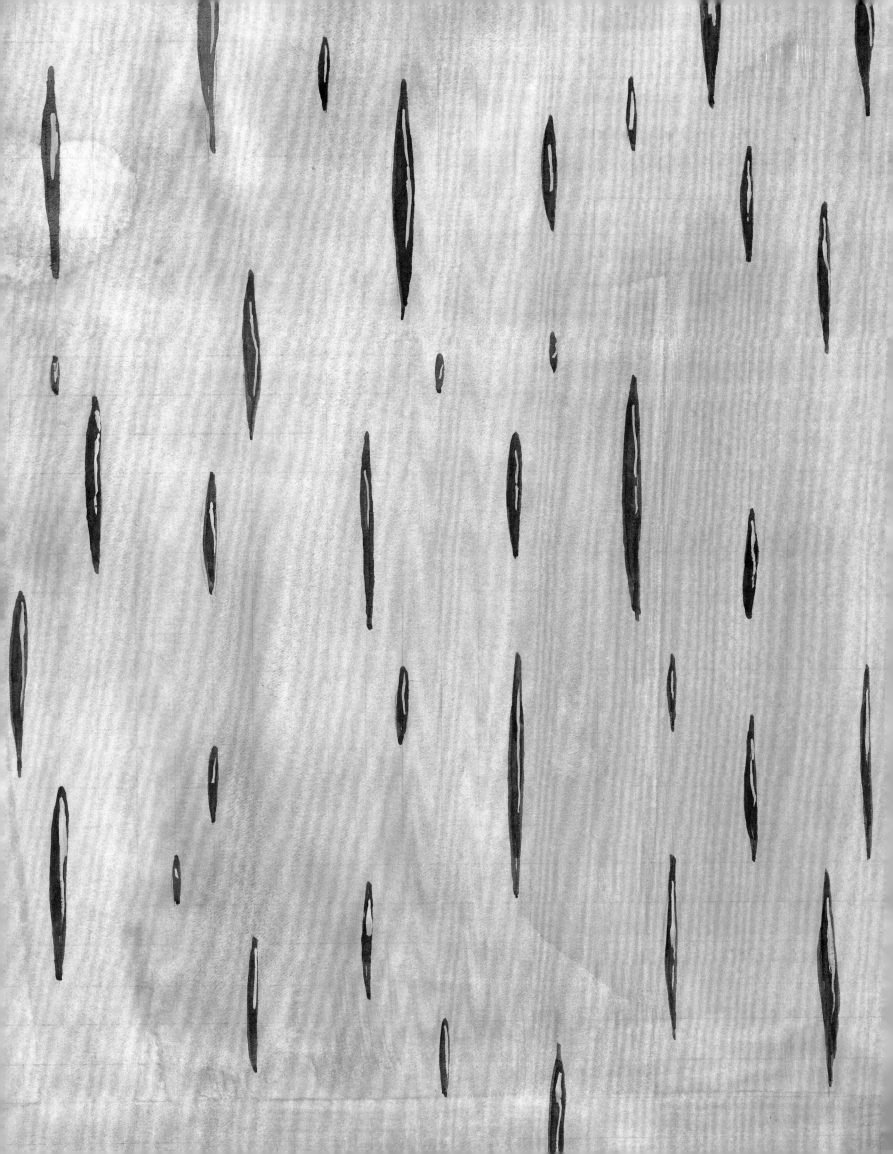

PATHS

Beauty can be found in unexpected places and in memories of sights that may resurface out of the blue, in ways that have nothing to do with the place or thing remembered. I love to play with selective memory, to act on a creative impulse that allows me to construct a fantasy or a fairy tale around an image. A detail from such a memory or sight can trigger a process of experimentation and end up in a design that is far removed from its origin, like a building block. The result can be quite startling. For instance, the sheen of the broken asphalt of a road I saw damaged from an earthquake on page 173 was translated into crystal embroidery on a dress on page 172. An asphalt road and an embroidered dress are unrelated, but in this case, it is the form that is affecting, not the meaning. Inspiring forms can be found anywhere. All you need to do is let your mind pick up salient features in the environment, features that will stand out given the right time, preference, season, or temperament. Forms tell a story that changes with each listener and with each viewer's subjectivity.

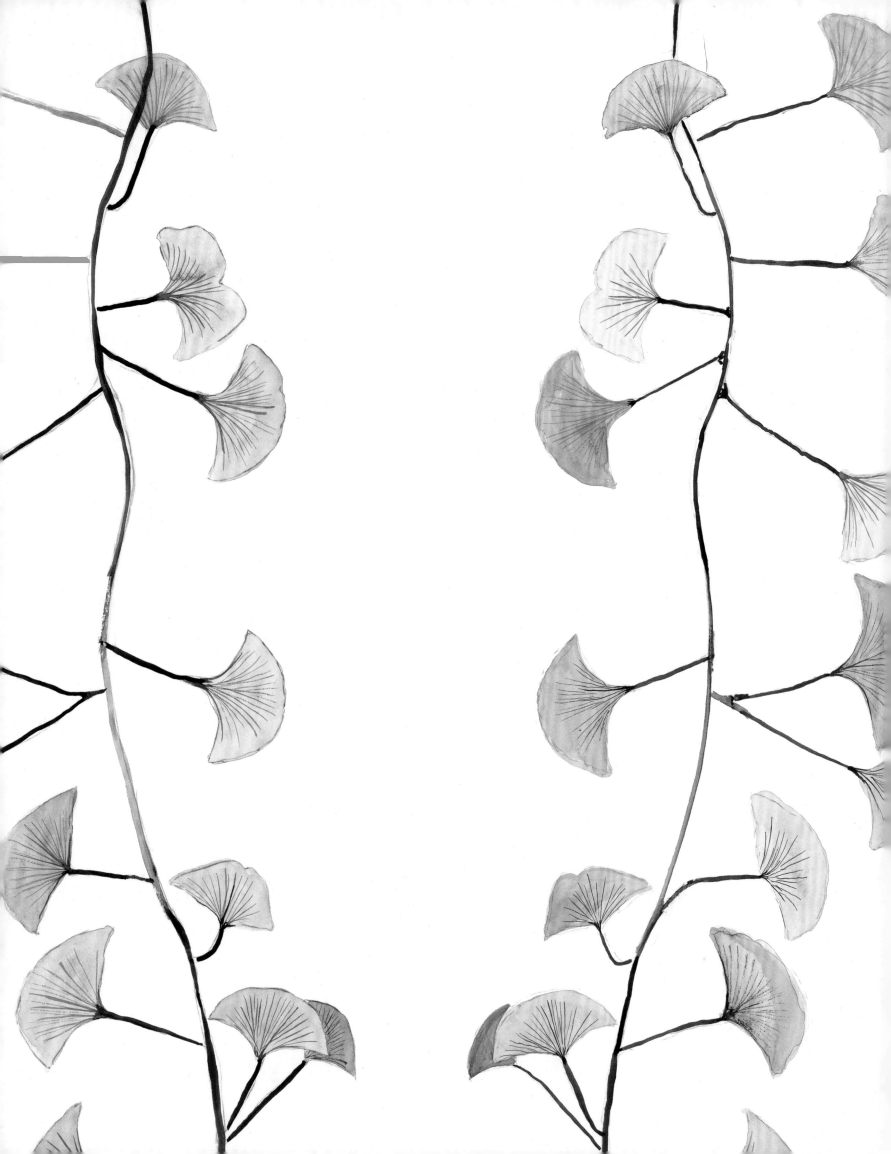

WINTER

IS STILL.
THERE IS LITTLE
LIGHT. LINES
ARE SHARP, AND
COLORS ARE MUTED.
JUST AS SPRING
COLORS ARE A
WATERCOLOR, SUMMER
A GOUACHE, AND AUTUMN
AN OIL PAINTING,
SO WINTER IS AKIN
TO AN ETCHING.

In winter,
you yearn for
light, color,
and warmth.
The colors of
winter fabrics
fluctuate between
the ones you
most long for—

reds and ochres that enhance the feeling of being enveloped in richness and luxury—and the actual look of nature in winter: muted grays and blues, whites, and blacks. Gold, yellows, and reds dominate the winter palette, suggesting warm fires that illuminate dark, long, cold nights and that counteract the chill of ice, the smell of snow, the sound of breaking twigs, and the lifeless stillness that is everywhere.

Ice has its beauty, too. Its stillness promises regeneration; its glasslike transparency is ethereal and reflects the sky with its range of blues, grays, and whites. Its counterpart in design are patterns that are more abstract than in other seasons, playing down nature's manifold, exuberant variety. At times, the design is minimalist, reflecting life at its minimum subsistence, as if concentrating all the energy that remains into just a few economical lines that are restful for the eyes and senses.

The winter world enters the realm of design as if it was a photograph, both still and framed; less observation is needed because nature is already an abstraction. Hues and saturation are almost nonexistent. An abstracted version of the winter landscape helps to overcome the cold—shiny jewels that recall the snow at night, gems that sparkle in winter light and multiply its pale, soft rays, and black that enhances contrasts. The slate is wiped clean in wintertime when designs are purer and less artificial; it is in this sense that winter design is essentially minimalist.

Winter is also a time when cities are important, since nature is dormant. New York, for instance, is the epitome of a winter city, perfect in its man-made structure for a time when the senses recoil from nature's impacts and resist the elements, when the body hides beneath protective garments, and when intellect prevails over instinct. Winter is less organic than other seasons and so are its designs, which are more constructed, more thoughtful and deliberate, and more concentrated than at other times. From color to black-and-white, winter interiors at once reflect the season and deflect from it.

RED

Red in winter is like a gift: Its warmth is embracing, generous, and sensuous. The fabric on page 180 is red paired with golds and dark browns. Its design is painterly and highly contrasted. Flower spikes appear in the midst of abstract shapes. The saturation of red is particularly satisfying in the winter. The fabric plays an enriching, warming role, similar to that of red objects and a red painting on a landing at the entrance of the room on page 181. I think red is perfect as an accent because of its intensity; as a very warm color, it gives off a feeling of heat, like a flame. It needs to be contained and surrounded, to appear in spots rather than on large surfaces. It complements other hues, whether warm or cold, and confers warmth on a white wall, spreading its power throughout the atmosphere. Red is a powerful primary color, not a combination of other colors. It is a statement that conveys strength. To use red is to be assertive and self-confident.

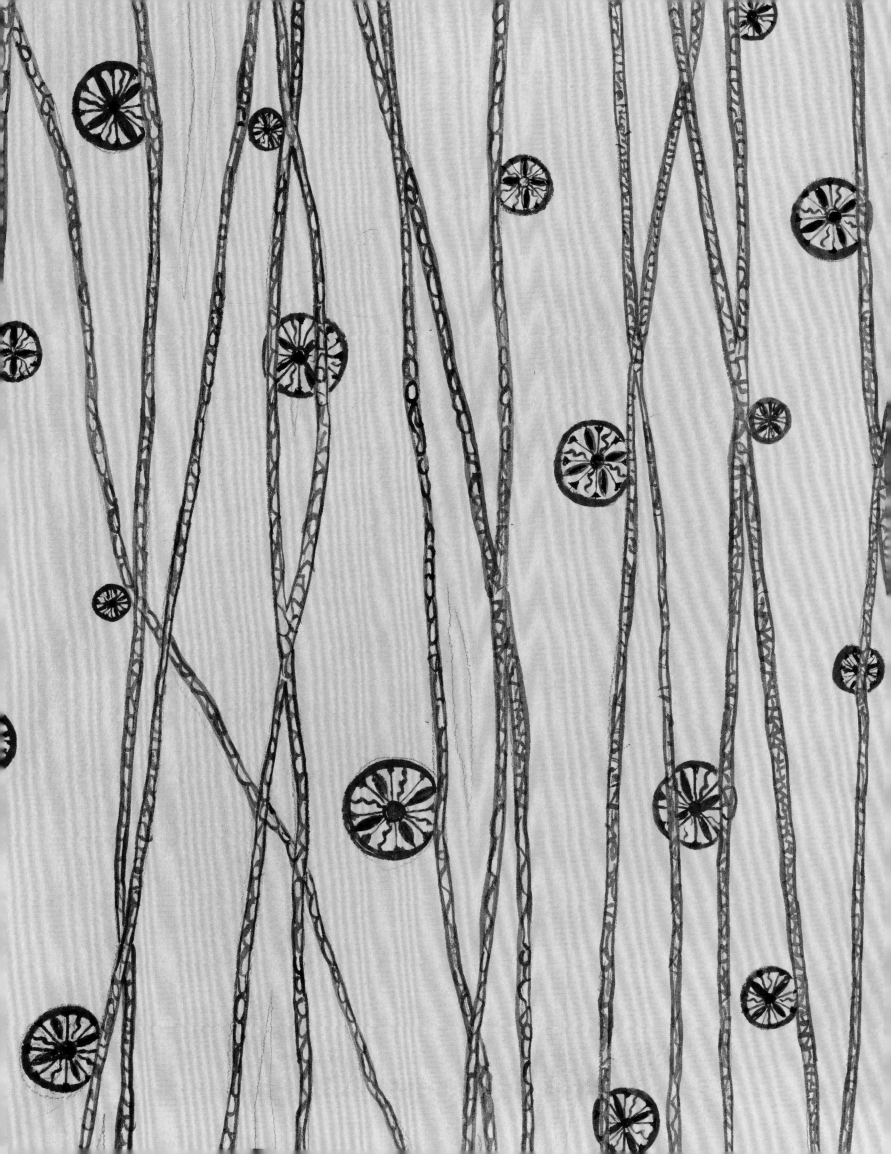

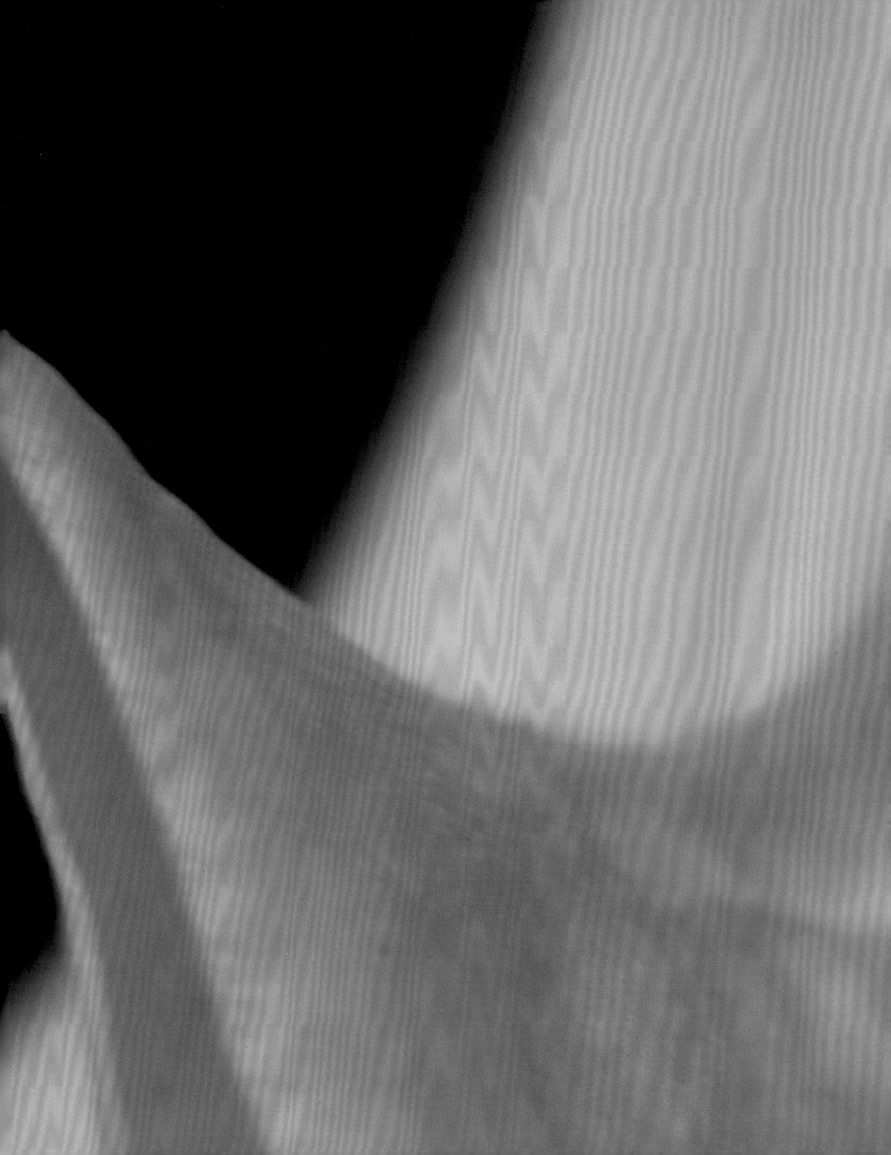

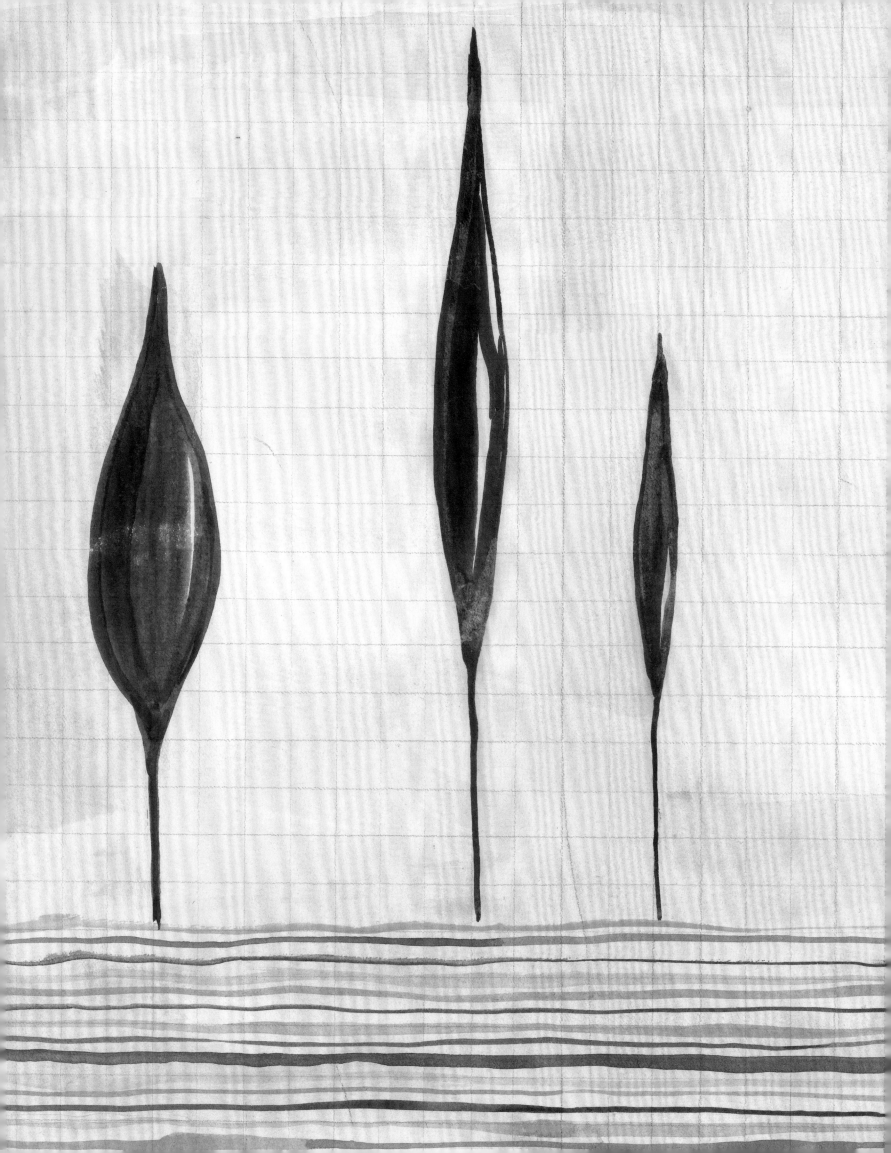

DARKNESS

A fragment of a flower petal on page 193 has its counterpart in a black fabric on its facing page speckled with white, icy tones that seem to have exploded randomly and dynamically, surrounded by patches of blue. The effect is that of ice that has crackled under our feet in the darkness, revealing the cold water beneath, or of exploded glass with both irregular and never repeated forms. The pattern is at once dynamic and entropic. The shapes are abstract, as is the flower petal, and in both cases, the light comes from a dark place. I like to play with the effect of darkness on light, and the inspiration here, again, came from an unexpected place: two universes, seasons, and atmospheres meeting in form rather than meaning. The cold colors confer on the fabric a sober elegance and atmosphere that one can achieve with pale flowers in a well-lit room, counteracting the darkness of winter.

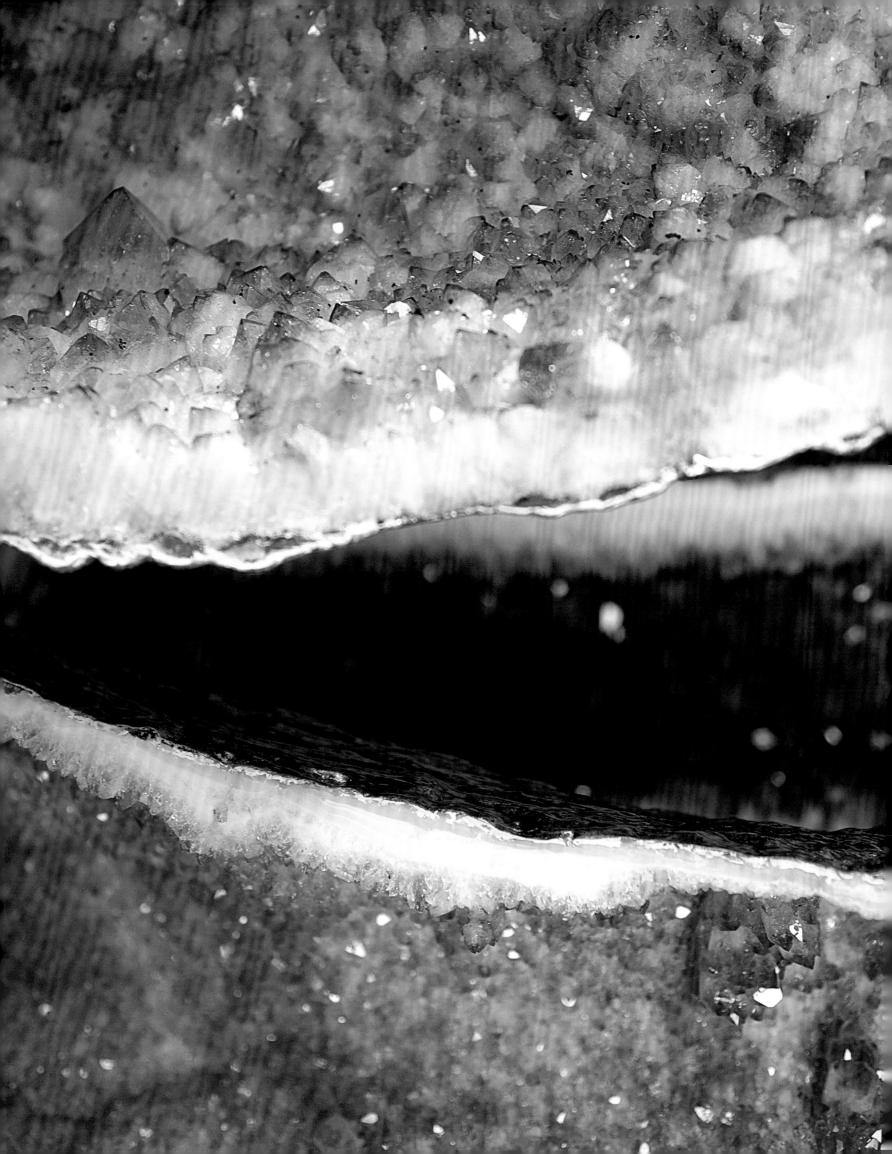

ORNAMENT

Corals, used in the fabric on page 205, are synonymous with summer. But out of their marine context, in an interior, they become sculpture. In that fabric two elements are in perfect harmony: the brown wood and the white dried marine life form. Similarly, while the fabric on page 204 uses my drop pattern, it no longer evokes water because it is a declension in browns, rather than blues or greens; the drop is abstracted from its original connotation, though its form gives the pattern a sense that one is grounded, as if falling to the earth. Here the drop has become essentially a wintry, earthy ornament, just like the coral. In both cases, a life is stilled into a beautiful object that is dry, white, and static, but whose shapes are potentially dynamic, like wintry, naked tree branches. The coral is delicate, while the silk of the fabric is ethereal. The white coral bears the same relation to the brown table as that of the drops to their muted background. A dry, restrained sense of luxury prevails. The whole effect is sophisticated, calming, and beautiful.

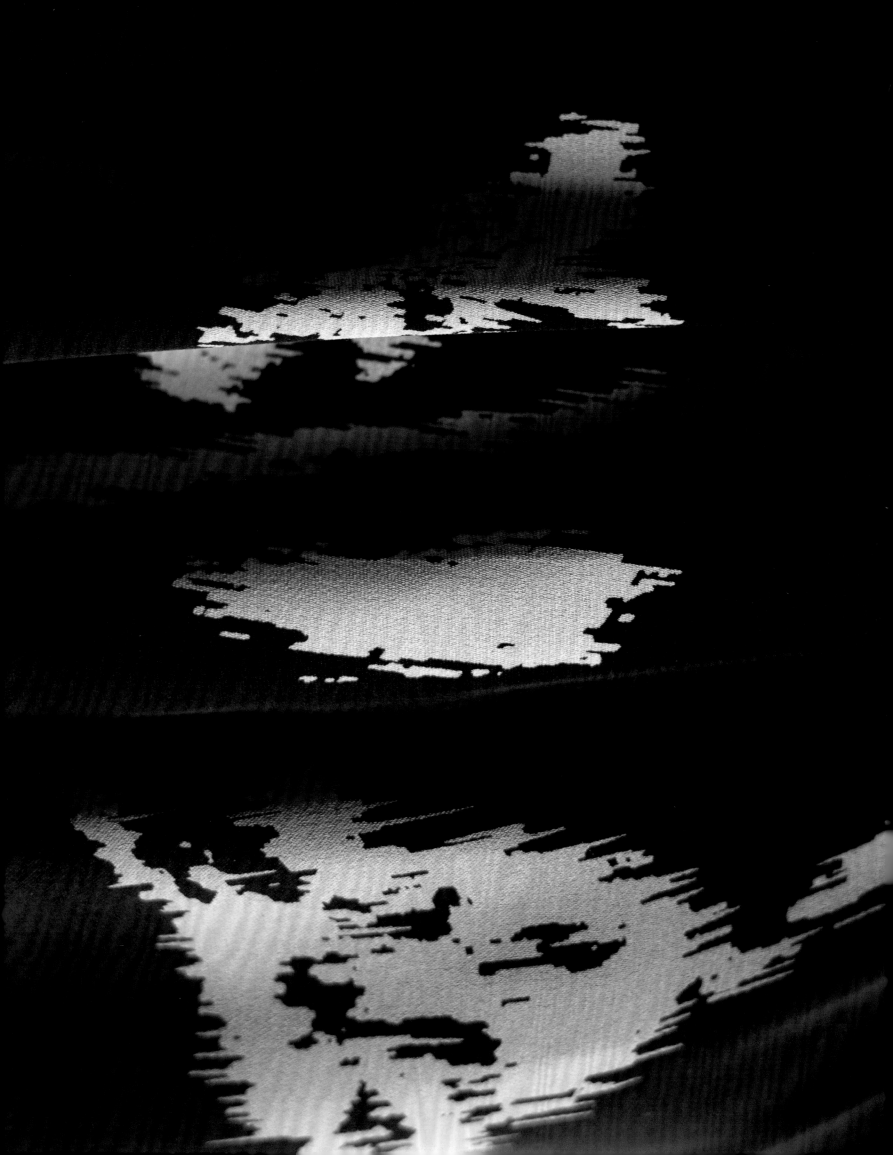

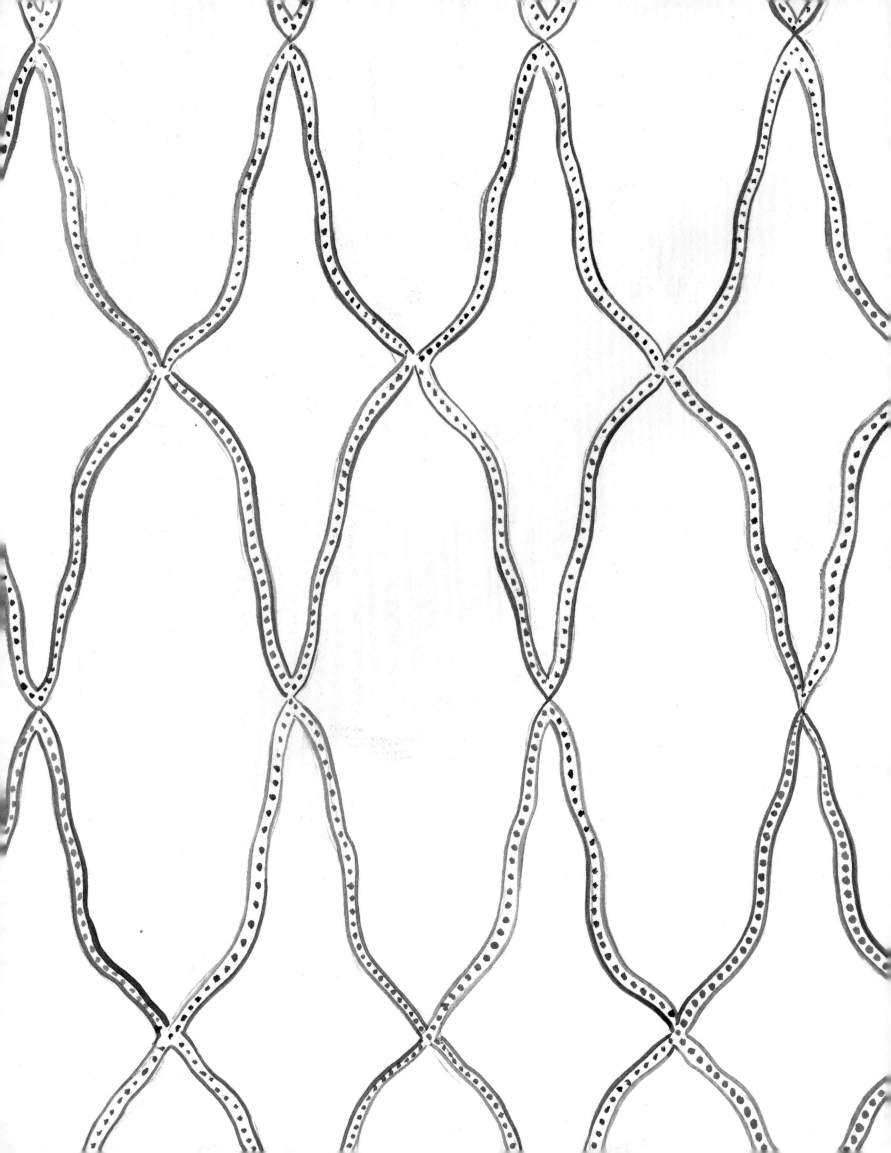

ICE

The absence of color prevails in the fabric on page 213, recalling the icy feeling of winter. All nature is still; there is no life. Abstracted shapes in the form of naked winter leaves are embroidered on an ice gray background. The fabric is a perfect counterpart to the winter landscape on page 212, which is unpolished by human hands, simply nature left on its own. The earth is iced and lined with snow, and the water is cold and flat. It is a perfect winter image of nature at rest, reminiscent, to my mind, of a fairy tale about an ice queen. The embroidery and glass beads on the fabric have a similar transparency that recalls water and cold air. There is something very sophisticated about the absence of color; it is evocative of something supremely precious, like a simple, gleaming diamond, while the interplay of shiny and matte on the fabric can enhance an interior by giving a sense of depth. The result is understated luxury.

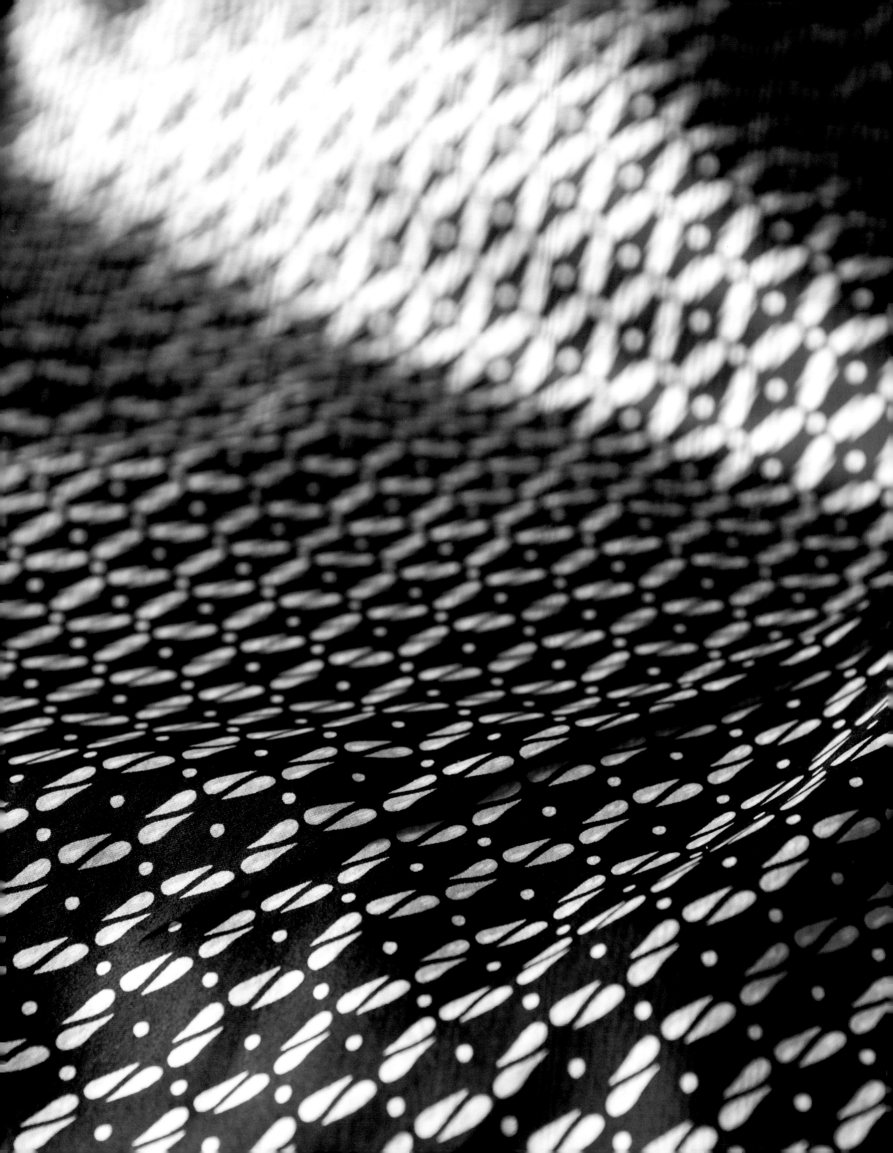

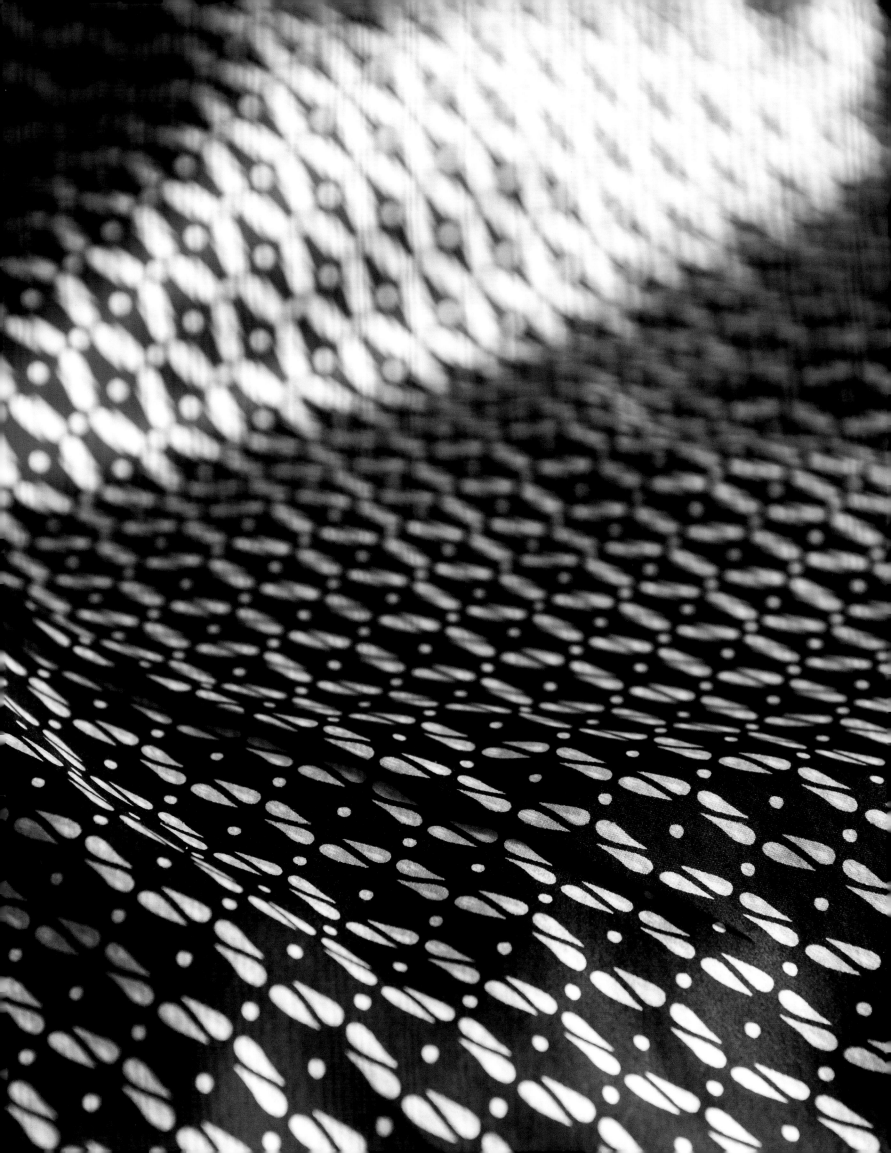

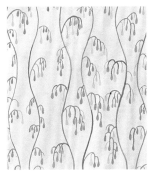

PAGE 2 WISTERIA, WATERCOLOR

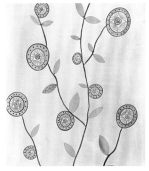

PAGE 16 TREE OF LIFE, WATERCOLOR

PAGE 20 SHELLS, PRINTED SILK SATIN

PAGE 21 POPPIES, PRINTED SILK CHIFFON

PAGE 22 ANGELS, PRINTED SILK SATIN

PAGE 23 LYNN CHADWICK SCULPTURE, LONDON HOUSE

PAGE 24 LILY POND, PRINTED SILK GEORGETTE

PAGE 25 FOREST, PRINTED SILK GEORGETTE

PAGE 26 LABYRINTH EMBROIDERY, CHENILLE

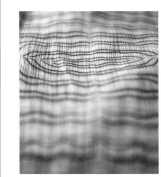

PAGE 27 LABYRINTH, PRINTED SILK CHIFFON

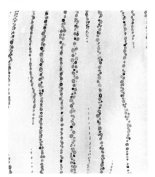

PAGE 29 WATERFALL, WATERCOLOR

PAGE 30 ZEBRANO, CUT VELVET

PAGE 31 MY BEDROOM ARMCHAIR BY ASHLEY HICKS. CUSHION MOON PRINTED COTTON SHAWL

PAGE 32 FAN LINEN

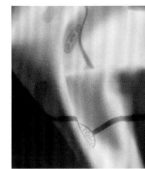

PAGE 33 TREE OF LIFE LINEN

PAGE 34-35 MEMORY HANDWOVEN RUG, LONDON

PAGE 36 GEMS, WATERCOLOR

PAGE 38 DINING ROOM HOUSE OF PAOLO È MARIA CATTANEO TUSCANY

PAGE 39 PEBBLE, WOOL AND SILK RUG

PAGE 40 LONDON HOUSE

PAGE 41 WATERLILY, LINEN

PAGE 42 SHADED HAND DYED CHIFFON

PAGE 43 PORTRAIT BY MARINA KARELLA BANUSTER AND CHAIR BY TOM DIXON

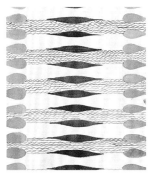

PAGE 45 SUNDERNAGAR WATERCOLOR

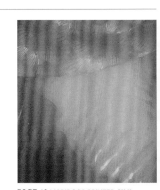

PAGE 46 MARIPOSA PRINTED SILK GEORGETTE

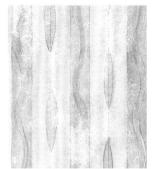

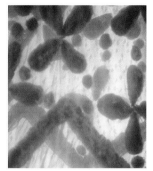

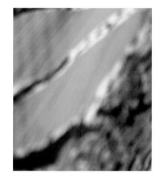

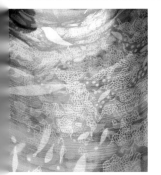

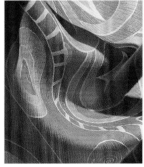

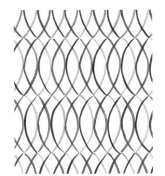

PAGE 82 INFINITY WATERCOLOR

PAGES 84–85 VIEW OF THE VESUVIO NAPLES

PAGE 86 HAY STUCK IN A FIELD OF AN ITALIAN PAINTER TUSCANY

PAGE 87 TREE OF LIFE, PRINTED LINEN

PAGE 88 TANGERINE, PRINTED SILK GEORGETTE

PAGE 89 KITCHEN OF AN ITALIAN PAINTER, TUSCANY

PAGE 90 KALI'S GAZE, WATERCOLOR

PAGE 92 LIBRARY OF AN ITALIAN PAINTER, TUSCANY

PAGE 93 ALMOND, PRINTED SILK JERSEY

PAGE 94 DANDELION, PRINTED LINEN

PAGE 95 TIBETAN ROOSTERS

PAGE 96 FLYING WINGS, PRINTED SILK COTTON

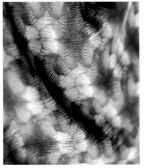

PAGE 97 MARIPOSA, PRINTED SILK CHIFFON

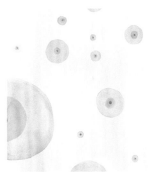

PAGE 98 ENERGY, WATERCOLOR

PAGE 100 - 101 DRAWING ROOM OF AN ITALIAN PAINTER, TUSCANY

PAGE 102 DROPS, PRINTED SILK CHIFFON

PAGE 103 PAOLO È MARIA CATTANEO'S HOUSE, TUSCANY

PAGE 104 FLAMES, PRINTED SILK JERSEY

PAGE 105 SITTINGROOM, RODMAN PRIMACK AND RUDY WEISSENBERG, LONDON

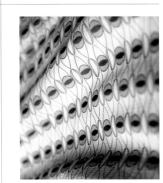

PAGES 106–107 SILK CHIFFON EYE DESIGN

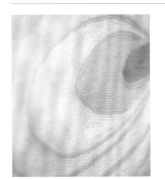

PAGE 108 AVALON CHAIN, STITCHED WOOL RUG

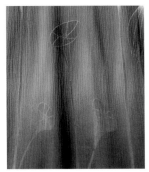

PAGE 109 ALICE, PRINTED SILK CHIFFON

PAGE 110 POLO, PRINTED COTTON

PAGE 111 BEDROOM, RODMAN PRIMACK AND RUDY WEISSENBERG LONDON, WALLS BY PETER DUNHAM DOG, SCULPTURE JEFF KOONS

PAGE 112 SMALL ALMOND, PRINTED COTTON

PAGE 113 ROSE GARDEN WITH TOMATOES, EMANUELE AND BENEDETTA TOURNON, TUSCANY

PAGE 115 HEARTS, WATERCOLOR

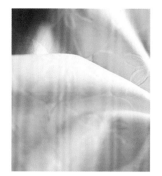

PAGE 116 SANDOLLARS, PRINTED COTTON

PAGE 117 ANTS ON A WALL, ROME

PAGE 118 WATERLILY, PRINTED SILK GEORGETTE

PAGE 119 LANDING WITH JACK PIERSON'S BLOOD MY HOUSE IN LONDON

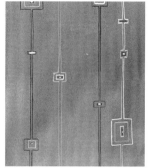

PAGE 120 CITIES, WATERCOLOR

PAGE 124 FEATHERS, PRINTED SILK GEORGETTE

PAGE 125 QUETZAL BIRD, RODMAN PRIMACK AND RUDY WEISSENBERG'S HOUSE LONDON

PAGE 126 SMOKEY QUARTZ ON SILK CHAIN-STITCHED SUNFLOWER CUSHION

PAGE 127 AQUAMARINE ON SILK CHAIN-STITCHED LIZARD CUSHION

PAGES 128–129 SARAH LUCAS SCULPTURE ON BAMBOO RUG, LONDON HOUSE

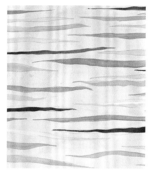

PAGE 130 BENARES, WATERCOLOR

PAGE 132 ROSES, PRINTED SATIN SILK

PAGE 133 AUTUMN CUSHIONS

PAGE 135 OAXACA FLOWER, WATERCOLOR

PAGE 136 SNOW FLAKES, PRINTED SILK JERSEY

PAGE 137 DINING ROOM SILK BEADED WALLS, MOBILE BY JULIA CONDON

PAGES 138–139 BENARES HAND WOVEN RUG, LONDON HOUSE

PAGE 140 INFINITY, CUT VELVET

PAGE 141 STAIRCASE WITH PATCHWORK FABRICS, VICTORIA FERNANDEZ'S HOUSE, LONDON

PAGE 142 VALENTINE, WATERCOLOR

PAGE 144 VICTORIA FERNANDEZ KITCHEN, LONDON

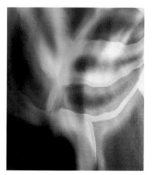

PAGE 145 AUTUMN, PRINTED SATIN SILK

PAGE 146 LIZARD, PRINTED SILK JERSEY

PAGE 147 OLIVE TREE, ITALIAN PAINTER'S GARDEN, TUSCANY

PAGES 148–149 OIL PORTRAIT OF ANGELICA BY JULIA CONDON, MY HOUSE LONDON

PAGES 150–151 PETER ADLER'S ROOM OF CURIOSITIES, LONDON

PAGE 153 WATERCOLOR

PAGE 154 BUTTERFLY DREAM, PRINTED SILK SATIN

PAGE 155 PETRIFIED WOOD FROM INDONESIA, PETER ADLER LONDON

PAGE 156 CHAIN PRINTED SILK CHIFFON

PAGE 157 TURKISH CERAMIC VASE ON AN ASHANTI FIGURATIVE STOOL, PETER ADLER, LONDON

PAGE 158 ELEMENTS WATERCOLOR

PAGE 160 IKAT, DROP WOVEN LINEN MIX

PAGE 161 PORTRAITS AND CUSHIONS MY LIBRARY LONDON

PAGE 162 ALMOND

PAGE 163 SULCIS IGLESIENTE, SARDEGNA, ITALY

PAGE 164 SATIN SILK GINKGO TREE

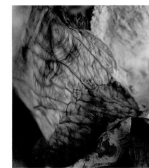

PAGE 165 DATURA PETALS

PAGE 167 FRAGILITY, WATERCOLOR

PAGE 168 AUTUMN, PRINTED SILK VELVET

PAGE 169 PAUL MC CARTHY'S PIG ON RIVERS HANDWOVEN WOOL RUG

PAGE 170 WATERCOLOR

PAGE 172 GLASS EMBROIDERY ON AUTUMN PRINTED SATIN SILK

PAGE 173 ROADWORKS, PALERMO, ITALY

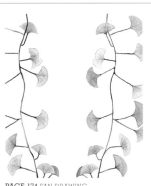

PAGE 174 FAN DRAWING

PAGES 178–179 MEXICAN HAND STITCHED EMBROIDERY

PAGE 180 DAMASK, PRINTED SILK JERSEY

PAGE 181 VIEW TO THE SITTING ROOM, MY HOUSE, LONDON

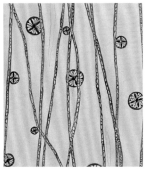

PAGE 183 POLO, WATERCOLOR

PAGE 184 FRENCH SILVER BROCADE

PAGE 185 ROMAN GLASS, MY HOUSE, LONDON

PAGE 186 SEQUIN ALMOND EMBROIDERY ON VELVET

PAGE 187 POND IN THE VALLE DI COMACCHIO, ITALY

PAGE 188 VENINI VASES IN MY LIBRARY LONDON

PAGE 189 INFINITY CUT VELVET

PAGES 190–91 MY SITTING ROOM, LONDON, CONSOLES BY ALLEGRA HICKS, DAY BED BY ASHLEY HICKS

PAGE 192 DUST, SATIN SILK

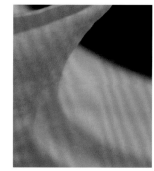

PAGE 193 DATURA PETAL

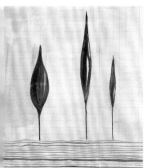

PAGE 194 WATERCOLOR

PAGE 196 QUARTZ

PAGE 197 LEAF CRISTAL BEADS, EMBROIDERY

PAGE 198 GOLD LEATHER BELT ON GOLD LINEN

PAGE 199 OIL PORTRAIT OF AMBROSIA BY JULIA CONDON, ORIEL HARVOOD CUP

PAGE 200 DRAGONFLY, CUT VELVET

PAGE 201 TABLESCAPE

PAGE 202 COLORWAYS OF CHAINS, PRINTED SILK GEORGETTE

PAGE 203 VICTORIA FERNANDEZ'S SITTING ROOM, LONDON

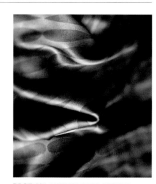

PAGE 204 WINTER DROPS, PRINTED SATIN SILK

PAGE 205 WHITE CORAL AND TABLE, GUY DE LOTBINIERE AND ANTY STOPPELLI'S HOUSE, LONDON

PAGE 207 WATERCOLOR

PAGE 208 DESERT FLOWER, DEVORÉ VELVET

PAGE 209 LANGLANDS AND BELL SCUPTURE, NUMFENBERG CHRIST AND CORAL ON A CONSOLE, MY SITTING ROOM, LONDON

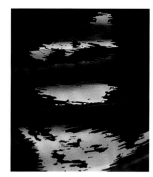

PAGE 210 SEBEL, PRINTED SILK JERSEY

PAGE 211 CACTUS

PAGE 212 VALLE DI COMACCHIO

PAGE 213 CRISTAL EMBROIDERY ON SILK GEORGETTE

PAGE 214 ICE, WATERCOLOR

PAGES 216-17 MUSIC, NOTES, PRINTED SILK SATIN

ACKNOWLEDGMENTS

PETER ADLER

NOGA ARIKHA

DEMETRA AND KARL AUERSPERG,

CHARLES AND LEONIE BOOTH-CLIBBORN

PAOLO AND MARIA CATTANEO,

VICTORIA FERNANDEZ

MARCO EGIZI

PATRICK KINMONTH

EMANUELE MASCIONI

ANTONIO MONFREDA

ROBERTO MOTTOLA

GIOVANNI SANJUST

CHRIS AND SUZANNE SHARP

MISO AND LALLO SIRIGNANO

ANTY STOPPELLI AND GUY DE LOTBINIERE

CARLO AND ROSY TONDATO

FEDERICA TONDATO

EMANUELE AND BENEDETTA TOURNON

FRANCESCO AND CELIA VENTURI

RUDY WEISSENBERG AND RODMAN PRIMACK